THE
THREE
ORDINARY
VOICES
OF GOD

MATTHEW KELLY

BLUE
sparrow

Copyright 2024 Kakadu, LLC.
PUBLISHED BY BLUE SPARROW
AN IMPRINT OF VIIDENT

To learn more about the author, visit:
www.MatthewKelly.com

Design by Todd Detering

ISBN: 978-1-63582-559-6 (hardcover)
ISBN: 978-1-63582-560-2 (eBook)
Audiobook available from Audible

10 9 8 7 6 5 4 3 2 1

Printed in the United States of America

TABLE OF CONTENTS

CHAPTER ONE: LET YOUR LIFE SPEAK

It's Possible to Mis-Live Your Life. 1

Let Your Life Speak 4

God Speaks to Everyone 6

The Three Voices: A Simple Introduction. 12

The Benefits of Listening to God's Voice 13

Personal Clarity 14

Clarity Leads to Engagement. 17

Will You Listen? 20

CHAPTER TWO: THE FIRST VOICE: NEEDS

Every Parent's Dream. 25

The First Voice: The Basics 29

The Four Aspects of the Human Person. 30

The Happiness Paradox 48

Getting What You Want Doesn't Make You Happy 50

God Loves Order. 53

God Wants You to Serve Powerfully 55

CHAPTER THREE: THE SECOND VOICE: TALENT

The Two Paths. 59

The Second Voice: The Basics 62

Everybody Is a Genius 64

Two Truths 68

Context Is a Beautiful Thing. 69

Unique and Universal Talent 72

CHAPTER FOUR: THE THIRD VOICE: DESIRES

The Power of Desire 77

The Third Voice: The Basics. 78

The Trivial Many vs. The Essential Few 80

From FOMO to JOMO. 82

Desire and the Four Aspects. 85

The Want Beyond the Want 93

CHAPTER FIVE: THE ULTIMATE DESIRE

That Nagging Feeling. 99

Your Heart's Dominant Desire 100

Unanswered Questions. 102

This Is How We Change Our Lives 103

The Cause of Our Pain. 105

The Only Tragedy. 106

The Unavoidable Appointment 111

EPILOGUE: COME TO THE QUIET

Fear the Right Things. 113

All the Other Voices 114

Come to the Quiet 116

Listening to God is an act of hopeful expectation.

Listening to God requires an open heart.

Listening to God requires us to set aside our personal preferences and agendas.

Listening to God involves letting go of our stubborn and prideful desire to do whatever we want.

Listening to God requires humility.

Listening to God is an act of surrender.

Will you listen?

CHAPTER ONE:
LET YOUR LIFE SPEAK

IT'S POSSIBLE TO MIS-LIVE YOUR LIFE

I must warn you to begin. I am compelled to tell you something terrifying. We all have fears, but most of us aren't terrified of what should petrify us.

I'm afraid of dogs. I was brutally attacked by a German Shepherd when I was a child. I'm a little afraid of flying. Never was before I had children. And I'm afraid of sharks when I swim in the ocean, even though I know statistically I have more of a chance of dying in a car accident, by drowning, from an accidental fall, or as a result of a medical error. Still I am afraid of sharks. Some people are afraid of snakes and spiders, others are afraid of the dark. But let me tell you what terrifies me.

I am petrified of mis-living my life. You can mis-live your life. Most people never consider it as a possibility, but it's true. You can mis-live your life. Let it sink in. It is possible.

We assume that all lives are well-lived. It isn't true. We deceive ourselves. Go to most funerals and you will hear about a well-lived life, even though everyone in attendance knows different.

A person's adolescence and early adulthood is often referred to as his or her "misspent youth." It is usually a playful reference to a period in a person's life when they engaged in activities considered unproductive, lazy, wasteful, and even dangerous in hindsight. The idea of a misspent youth is often laughed off, but the truth is, there are a good number of people who engaged in exactly the same behavior who are in prison or dead as a result.

You can mis-live your life.

The disturbing truth is you don't even need to do something significantly egregious. You don't need to become a drug addict or murder someone to mis-live your life. You can do it in the most mundane and ordinary ways. It can happen so subtly that the people around you wouldn't even notice, because you have most likely surrounded yourself with people mis-living their lives in exactly the same ways.

All it takes is the consistent application of mediocrity, laziness, procrastination, obsession with material possessions, and self-centeredness.

We speak of people who have lost their way and lives that have gone off the rails. But do you ever consider that you have lost your way, that your life is off the rails, and that you are mis-living your life? That's the biggest mistake: Not even considering the possibility. Assuming that it won't happen to you.

But perhaps the most heartbreaking part of all this is that by mis-living your life you will never get to see or experience the life God envisioned for you. You miss out on the life God wanted to give you. That's heartbreaking.

We often wander carelessly through life as if a well-lived life were guaranteed. It isn't.

What does it mean to mis-live your life? It is the opposite of a well-lived life. It means to live poorly. It means to lead a life marked by wasted potential and misaligned with all that is good, true, just, and noble. I'll say it again: You can mis-live your life. But most people never think about it. They wander aimlessly through life, unconsciously assuming that all lives are well-lived, even though everybody knows people who have mis-lived their lives.

Have you ever mis-lived an hour? An afternoon? A day? I have. I have mis-lived too many. So many. I have mis-lived hours and afternoons. I have mis-lived moments and I have mis-lived months.

The problem is, put enough of those mis-lived days together and you will find yourself on the wrong side of a life well-lived. And that is a frightening thing. Finding your way back from such a place can be daunting. It is beyond difficult, I won't lie. But it is possible. So, if that is where you find yourself, please do not lose hope.

How do you find your way back from mis-lived days and weeks, or even years? It is simple but not easy. It is done one choice at a time. And whether your day has gone adrift or your life, begin now, without delay. Rectify your life immediately.

A well-lived life is built the same way a mis-lived life is built—one choice at a time. Every choice builds character or erodes character. Make your next choice one that belongs in a well-lived life. It's amazing how one good choice can shift the momentum of your day. Do you need to make a shift?

You can ruin your life. Ask people. Everyone's seen ruined lives. They are tragic and pathetic, filled with regret and often cliché. And most people only realize this at the end.

We cannot avoid our appointment with death. Death comes to us all eventually. And when death approaches, the person you have become meets the person you could have been. This is a humbling encounter. Don't wait for it. Meet with the person you are capable of becoming for a few minutes each day. The more time you spend in these meetings the less you will fear death. Use your thoughts, words, choices, and actions to close the gap between who you are today and who you are capable of being. This is the path that leads to a deeply fulfilling life.

We live or mis-live our lives one choice at a time. Some choices are full of goodness and life, others are nothing but death and destruction. Some choices create chaos and confusion, others give birth to clarity and order. Build your tomorrow with your choices today. Envision the person God created you to become and build toward that vision of your future self—one choice at a time.

You can mis-live your life. If you pause for long enough to think about it, if you allow the possibility to sink in, it is disturbing, terrifying actually. But here is the beautiful truth—you can shift the momentum of your life with a single choice.

The choice to listen to the voice of God is such a choice. Decide here and now, today, to open your heart and listen to the three ordinary voices of God. If you do, I promise, God will use the needs, talents, and desires he created you with to fill your life with passion and purpose.

LET YOUR LIFE SPEAK

Eight hundred years ago, Saint Francis of Assisi wrote, "Preach the Gospel at all times, and only when necessary use words." Four hundred years later, this was no doubt the inspiration for George Fox, the founder of the Quaker movement, when he wrote, "Let your life preach." This saying has evolved over the past four hundred years into *let your life speak.*

Let your life speak implies that your life might not speak. That isn't the case. The truth is this: You don't have a choice. Your life speaks whether you let it or not. Your actions speak and your inaction speaks. The only choice you have in this matter surrounds this question: What is your life saying to the world?

Is your life whispering wisdom to the world? Or is your life cursing at the world and everyone in it? Is your life the holy ranting of a prophet? Is your life praising the goodness of others or gossiping about them behind their backs?

If you had to summarize what your life is saying in one word, what word would you use? Love, generosity, thoughtful, responsible, irresponsible, light, dark, righteous, sarcastic, hypocritical, degenerate, goodness, kindness, selfish, thoughtless, careless, anxious, depressed, truth, beauty, wisdom?

Your life is speaking.

At work people have reputations. "He is always late." "She is always helpful." "She is always the first to leave." "He's a genius." "He is such a hard worker." "She is so committed." "He can't be serious." The list goes on. Everybody has a personal brand at work. Some are acquired intentionally. Most by default.

How would the people who know you well describe you? What would they say?

"He's the most sarcastic person I've ever known."

"She's the most generous person in the world."

"He is very hard to get to know."

"She is constantly gossiping."

There are plenty of workshops and college classes that ask students to write their own eulogies or obituaries. These usually include personal and professional achievements, key relationships, life lessons, values, and how the person hopes to be remembered. It's a fine exercise often dismissed as trite or cliché by those who forget that clichés become clichés by containing some element of universal wisdom. The virtue of this exercise is to develop a vision of the life we wish to live, so as to align our thoughts, words, and actions with that vision each day.

Writing a personal mission statement is another powerful exercise. I know that some people may dismiss this as merely "self-help" or "less than," but that would be a mistake. If anything, we should take it even more seriously than those who harness such tools to seek worldly outcomes.

It would seem to me that having a crisp and clear description of the life we aspire to live, that can be called to mind throughout the day to guide the decisions that form your character and life, would be of significant and practical advantage.

One sentence. Two at most. A personal mission statement. Write it down. Repeat it to yourself in your mind, over and over, throughout the day. And before too long, you will notice it guiding your thoughts, words, and actions.

Visualize the life you wish to live, the person God is calling you to become, and how you wish to be known and remembered. This will allow your life to speak a crisp and clear message. But how can such personal clarity be achieved? By learning to listen to the voice of God.

Letting your life speak is a beautiful idea. But in order for your life to speak a profound message it is first necessary to allow God to speak into your life.

Your personal mission statement can only be composed with his wise counsel.

And that's what we are going to learn to do: Listen to God speak to you each and every day of your life. And it will change everything.

I know it may seem impossible, but I assure you, it isn't. In fact, once you learn how to listen to God's voice in the moments of your day, you will understand why you made the mistakes you made along the way, and you will wonder how you ever lived without his intimate guidance.

GOD SPEAKS TO EVERYONE

The question isn't, "Does God speak to people?" The question is, "Is anybody listening?" A cursory glance around society would lead anyone to conclude, "Fewer and fewer."

Before Moses led the Israelites out of slavery in Egypt, the Biblical narrative in the Book of Exodus reveals that God spoke to Moses through a burning bush. After the Israelites had escaped slavery and Egypt, Moses ascended Mount Sinai to ask God for further instruction and direction. God gave Moses the most universal instruction and direction humanity had ever received. This event is known as "The Giving of the Law" and the fruit of this encounter with God was the Ten Commandments.

I have asked it before, and I will ask it again: How would our nation and world be different if everyone strived to live these Ten Commandments? Turn on the evening news tonight and story after story contains a blatant violation of at least one of the ten.

Take a moment and reflect on the wisdom, clarity, and order that each commandment yearns to bathe our lives and society with.

The Ten Commandments
1. I am the Lord your God; you shall have no other gods before me.
2. You shall not take the name of the Lord your God in vain.
3. Keep holy the Sabbath.
4. Honor your father and your mother.
5. You shall not kill.
6. You shall not commit adultery.
7. You shall not steal.
8. You shall not bear false witness against your neighbor.
9. You shall not covet your neighbor's wife.
10. You shall not covet your neighbor's goods.

God speaks to us. He has been speaking to us from the beginning. There is a temptation to think, "Well, God spoke to people in the Bible, and he spoke to some medieval saints and mystics, but he doesn't speak to me." Wrong.

To understand how wrong that assumption is, consider this: The most common preface to any sentence in the Bible is, "God said..."

In his Letter to the Hebrews, Saint Paul affirmed this truth: "In the past God spoke to our ancestors through the prophets at many times and in various ways, but in these last days he has spoken to us by his

Son whom he appointed heir of all things and through whom also he made the universe. The Son is the radiance of God's glory and the exact representation of his being sustaining all things by his powerful word." (Hebrews 1:1-3)

God spoke to Moses, he spoke to Noah, he spoke to Mary. God spoke to Adam and Eve, Abraham, Isaac, Jacob, Joshua, Samuel, David, Solomon, Elijah, Isaiah, Jeremiah, Ezekiel, and the other prophets.

God chose different ways to speak to different people. He spoke to Moses through the burning bush.

God spoke to many others through dreams. He spoke to Pharaoh through dreams. He spoke to Joseph when Mary was betrothed to him through dreams. And he spoke to Jacob, Solomon, and Daniel through dreams.

God spoke to many more through his angels. He spoke to Abraham and Sarah using three angelic visitors who proclaimed God's favor had come to rest upon them despite their old age. Two angels visited Lot and his family. An angel of the Lord appeared to Hagar to speak of her future and that of her son Ishmael. Jacob wrestled with an angel and exclaimed, "I have seen God face to face." The angel of God manifested as a pillar to guide the Israelites through the wilderness. An angel spoke to Gideon and to Samson's parents. The prophet Daniel had a series of encounters with angels, who provided him with powerful visions and accurate interpretations. And, of course, the angel Gabriel spoke to Zechariah and Mary to announce the birth of John the Baptist and the conception of Jesus.

God—in the form of Jesus—even spoke to devils and evil spirits. Do you really think he hasn't been speaking to you?

Words are among the fundamental tools of life. Speech too. They are also the tools that God chose to use very powerfully throughout salvation history. God used words to create: "Then God said, 'Let there

be light' and there was light. And God saw the light, that it was good."
(Genesis 1:3) "Then God said, 'Let the waters under the heavens be
gathered together into one place, and let the dry land appear' and it
was so." (Genesis 1:9) And, of course, Jesus himself is referred to as
"The Word."

Divine Revelation is the direct communication of truth to humanity. We believe God has most fully revealed himself to us through Jesus
Christ, the Alpha and the Omega, the Word of God Incarnate. The
Divine Revelation takes two forms: Scripture and Tradition. Both are
an integral part of Revelation, and God speaks to us through both.

God is the ultimate Father desperate to speak with his children.
He wants to lead and guide us, console and comfort us, coach and
protect us, be at our side when things are amazing and cling to our
side when our worlds seem to be crushing in upon us.

Our God infuses us with compassion that can put an end to hate,
with generosity that can eradicate greed, and with the wisdom and
courage to put our fears and sorrows in their rightful place.

Most people have never met this kind of earthly father or heavenly
Father, and it is past time we did something about that.

And, of course, God speaks to us through the woman he chose to be
the mother of his Son.

In 1531, Mary, the Mother of God, appeared as a young woman to
an indigenous peasant named Juan Diego. She asked him to build a
church, but that seemed impossible to him. Mary continued to appear
to him and on December 12, she instructed him to gather roses from
a hillside and present them to the bishop as a sign. Juan Diego gathered the roses in an old tilma (a simple indigenous cloak). When he
later unfolded the cloak for the bishop, a stunning image miraculously
appeared on the tilma. It was an image of Mary, known today as Our
Lady of Guadalupe, Queen of Mexico, and Patroness of the Americas.

The tilma has been examined several times by scientists and all manner of miracles have been discovered. You can view the tilma in Mexico City, where twenty million people visit each year.

In 1858, Mary appeared to a young peasant girl named Bernadette near a grotto in Lourdes, France. She came as God's messenger. It has been a place of faith and healing ever since. More than two hundred million pilgrims have visited Lourdes since Mary first appeared to Bernadette.

In 1917, Mary appeared to three young shepherd children in Fatima, Portugal. The children had many conversations with Mary, during which she invited them to pray for all those who were lost and suffering in the world. She also performed miracles for everyone present to see, most notably The Miracle of the Sun, which was witnessed by more than 70,000 people and reported in dozens of secular newspapers around the world. Five million people visit Fatima each year yearning to be close to Jesus and his mother.

God is constantly communicating with humanity. The question remains: Are we listening?

God speaks to us through the Scriptures, the Sacraments, Tradition, other people, situations and circumstances, dreams, visions, apparitions, and prophecy. Sometimes he speaks to us through our emotions and intuition, through our pain and suffering, and as we will soon discover, God speaks to every single person every single day using three ordinary voices: needs, talents, and desires. He speaks to us in the depths of our souls.

God goes to heroic lengths to guide, warn, coach, and direct his children. Not just in the past, but here and now, today.

More than that, it seems that God will use any and all means necessary to get a message through to us. The Old Testament records God speaking through a burning bush (Exodus 3), a thick cloud

(Exodus 19:9) and in a gentle whisper (1 Kings 19:12).

But that's all in the past. This is your moment. Here and now. You are standing at the crossroads of your life. And our God loves free will, so you get to choose.

When Moses was about to die, he said to Joshua and the people of Israel, "I set before you today life and prosperity, death and adversity." (Deuteronomy 30:15) Moses couldn't choose for Joshua any more than God could choose for Moses.

Will you choose life and prosperity or death and adversity?

How will you know which path leads to life and prosperity and which path leads to death and adversity? Great question. Glad you asked it. You will know by listening to the voice of God. By allowing the God of all creation to speak into the moments and circumstances of your life.

There's a thirteen-year-old girl on the other side of town and she's in danger. Her Father knows she's in danger, but she won't answer her phone. That Father is desperate to get a hold of his daughter. Imagine his anguish.

There's a thirty-five-year-old man about to make the worst decision of his life. His Father knows what his son is thinking of doing, and he is desperate to talk to his son, help him to see the mistake he is about to make, and the tsunami of consequences one stupid choice can set in motion. But his son won't accept any of his invitations. The Father's anguish is monumental.

You're the thirteen-year-old girl thinking of doing something that will alter her life in ways she cannot begin to imagine. It will reshape how she thinks about herself, it will change the way she speaks to herself, it will impact her mental health and her physical health—but she is too young to see any of that. God equipped her with a gentle voice within, it is a voice of goodness and wisdom, and it is a voice her Father

God desperately hopes she will listen to tonight.

God is the ultimate Father who yearns to speak into the lives of his children. He will go to unfathomable lengths to communicate with us. Do you really think he's not going to speak to you?

God the Father yearns deeply to communicate with you. He is the Father who wants good things for you more than you want them for yourself. Will you pause the insanity of your life for a few minutes each day and listen to him?

THE THREE VOICES: A SIMPLE INTRODUCTION

There will be some who will persist in the "God doesn't speak to me" attitude. Just as there are people who persist in the "I have no talents" attitude, even though they clearly have the ability to make a huge difference in other people's lives and that is an extraordinary talent.

The title of this book refers to three ordinary voices of God. They are ordinary in the sense that we encounter them in the ordinary moments of our lives. But these three voices are ordinary like people are ordinary—there is no such thing. C.S. Lewis observed, "There are no ordinary people. You have never talked to a mere mortal. Nations, cultures, arts, civilizations—these are mortal, and their life is to ours as the life of a gnat. But it is immortals whom we joke with, work with, marry, snub and exploit—immortal horrors or everlasting splendors."

There is no such thing as an ordinary person and there is no such thing as an ordinary voice of God. When God speaks it is a gift of inestimable value.

One of the many things that makes our faith astounding is found in the reality that God has made himself known to us. Not as a distant, anonymous, unknowable God, but as an intimate God who yearns to share in every triumph and tragedy of our lives, and even more so, in our mundane daily routines and rituals.

This is where we find the three "ordinary" voices most active. These voices are: need, talent, and desire.

God created you with needs. If you don't eat you will die. And so, in a loving and astoundingly practical way, when you hear the call of legitimate need, you hear the gentle voice of God guiding you.

God has endowed you with certain talents. They are different in aggregate than those he has endowed your sister, best friend, or parents with. He has given you these talents to equip you to carry out the mission he envisioned for you before the beginning of time. He speaks to you through these talents at each stage of your life.

God has placed the roaring flame of desire within you. It can be harnessed to accomplish and experience many things, but as we will discover, the more we listen to the voice of desire the more we come to understand that we have one desire that reigns above all others.

These three voices will teach us many things, but first and foremost, they will demonstrate that God speaks to you. And the more we understand how God speaks to us through our needs, talents, and desires, the more we will understand that he has been speaking to us our whole lives.

THE BENEFITS OF LISTENING TO GOD'S VOICE

The benefits of listening to the voice of God are vast and varied. Direction and wise counsel, peace and comfort, spiritual growth, empowerment to serve, union with God and a growing awareness of God's presence throughout the day, to name a few. But there are two we will focus on today. They are immensely practical. I have found them exceedingly helpful during times of chaos and confusion. And, in many cases, they will help you to know and understand yourself as if for the first time.

When I listen to the voice of God and strive to carry out his will,

I become focused, energized, and invigorated. When I turn my back on God, or run from his will and ways, I become distracted, depleted, and lethargic. All the energy and enthusiasm drain from my life.

I have been observing this pattern in myself for more than thirty years and encourage you to begin to observe these qualities in yourself.

When I am *not* focused, energized, and invigorated, there is a good chance I am not listening to God's voice, which means I am taking direction from someone other than God, and that is usually dangerous. It sometimes means the voice I am listening to is my own and that my selfishness has run amok. But most of the time, if I am not listening to the voice of God, I have simply fallen into the trap of allowing many voices to ping pong me back and forth into a state of confusion. The problem is, listening to all those voices and trying to work out which one to follow is exhausting, and when we are exhausted we make poor decisions.

The benefits of listening to God's voice in your life versus listening to a bunch of people who know almost nothing about nothing should be obvious. But when we get caught up in the speed and noise of the world, we get disoriented and start to think that those people are experts. They aren't. God is the expert on you and your life.

PERSONAL CLARITY

Personal clarity is an amazing thing. It is also incredibly attractive. When you meet someone who has a piercing sense of personal clarity it can be mesmerizing.

So, let's explore one of the most astounding and practical benefits of listening to God's voice: personal clarity.

What is personal clarity? Personal clarity is a spiritual state of awareness that allows you to see clearly who you are, what you are here for, what matters most, and what doesn't matter at all.

This clarity comes from collaborating with God to firmly establish your priorities, values, and goals.

When we are living in a state of personal clarity we are able to lay our heads on our pillows at night knowing that who we are, where we are, and what we are doing makes sense. And that is no small thing.

Most people's lives don't make sense to themselves.

Most people live anxiously in a cloud of confusion.

Most people have very little personal clarity.

Most people make very little effort to listen to the voice of God in their lives.

And sadly, tragically, most people have never been taught how to escape or step beyond these miserable and stressful states. This book is designed to liberate you from a life that doesn't make sense to you, by helping you acquire the staggering personal clarity that comes from learning how to listen to the voice of God.

People with great personal clarity have taken time to answer five of life's biggest questions. We all wrestle with these five questions throughout our lives. The great thinkers of every age have discussed and debated them, and now it is your turn.

Who am I?

What am I here for?

Where am I going?

What matters most?

What matters least?

The simple answers to these questions are:

Who am I? A child of God, uniquely and wonderful made.

What am I here for? You are here to love God and neighbor. God has assigned you a specific mission that will allow you to accomplish all this while at the same time becoming all that he created you to be.

Where am I going? You are a pilgrim. All pilgrimages are sacred journeys to sacred destinations. Your destination is God, in heaven, for eternity.

What matters most? People were made to be loved and things were made to be used. You are not here to solve the problems; the problems are here to make you holy.

Who you become is infinitely more important than what you do, have, accomplish, or buy.

What matters least? Anything that becomes an obstacle between you and God, you and loving others, or you and your God-given mission.

As you develop clear and concise answers to these questions, you get really, really good at something most people on the planet are really, really bad at: saying no. Learning to say no to anyone and anything that stands between you and God's plan for your life is a crucial life skill. It makes sense, but most people have never been taught this.

Learn to say no to anything and everything that is too small for you. The result: You become decisive. This is no small thing. This is the beginnings of becoming a great decision maker. God has so many dreams for you, and one of those dreams is for you to become a phenomenal decision maker. Listening to the voice of God leads to personal clarity, and personal clarity leads to great decisions.

Personal clarity is a beautiful thing. It will change every aspect of your life. The techniques in this book will help you develop it, but everything begins with prayer. So, I encourage you to ask God to give you personal clarity and remind you of one of Jesus' promises: "Ask and it will be given to you; seek and you will find; knock and the door will be opened to you. For everyone who asks receives; the one who seeks finds; and to the one who knocks, the door will be opened." (Matthew 7:7-8)

When was the last time you really asked, sought, knocked? It's time to ask God to flood your heart, mind, and soul with clarity.

CLARITY LEADS TO ENGAGEMENT

It is impossible to be disengaged and happy. We encounter disengaged people every day. Most of the time they don't understand the true purpose and value of what they are doing.

The miserable checkout operator at the grocery store probably thinks the purpose of work is to make money. He wouldn't be alone. Millions and millions of people miserable at work today think the main reason they go to work is to make money. There's nothing wrong with making money. It's necessary, but it's not enough.

Making money to sustain ourselves and support our families is noble. It is one of the reasons we work. But it isn't enough to make work fulfilling, not if you are making fourteen dollars an hour and not if you are making $400,000 a year. It may be hard to believe for the person making fourteen dollars an hour, but people who are lazy and have bad attitudes are still miserable when they are making $400,000 a year.

Making money isn't the primary reason to work. Making money is secondary. It's necessary, but still secondary.

The primary purpose of work is that it helps you become a-better-version-of-yourself. Working hard, striving for excellence, paying attention to the details of your work, and serving other people joyfully transforms you into a better human being. The primary value of work is that it helps you develop character—and character is destiny.

The character of someone who refuses to work hard, settles for mediocrity in everything, neglects the details of his work, and begrudgingly serves people while spreading the misery of his chosen attitude will be very poor indeed. What quality of friend would this person be? How would all this impact his mental and physical health? Would you want this person as your neighbor? And what woman would say, "This is the man of my dreams, I feel confident that he will proactively partner with me to maximize the opportunities that come our way and mitigate the problems we encounter"?

"Character is destiny." It was true 2,500 years ago when the Greek philosopher Heraclitus first observed it, and it is true and observable today.

And above all this, there is yet a higher purpose and calling to work. Work is also a form of prayer. Each hour of work offered to God for a specific person or intention has infinite value and power.

This beautiful and practical way to approach work has never been taught to most people, even those earnestly striving to live the faith. Each hour of work has infinite value.

Each hour of work is an hour of prayer. This simple, and yet astoundingly profound idea reveals the higher meaning and purpose of work. But a sad realization quickly descends upon us: Most people have never been taught to approach work this way. Meanwhile, every new generation that enters the workforce demands that their work be more intrinsically meaningful, while being completely ignorant to their own ability to infuse their work with astounding meaning.

The second practical benefit of listening to the voice of God is engagement.

Engagement is a thing of beauty. To see a young student deeply immersed in her work is inspiring. That's engagement. To see a football team working together cohesively toward a common goal, rather than a collection of individual egos obsessed with personal success, that lifts our spirits. It's inspiring to see a married couple working through a tough time. It demonstrates that it is possible, and witnessing always brings hope to many.

Engagement is attractive and inspiring, but human beings are rarely 100% engaged. In fact, we are constantly, moment to moment, engaging and disengaging in everything we do.

You may be 87% engaged at work today and 62% tomorrow. You

might be quick to argue that your engagement never falls that low at work. But you get a common cold, not cancer, just a cold. You still go to work because there is a lot going on. What happens next? You disengage. You say to yourself, "What projects absolutely have to get done today? Everything else can wait." You've disengaged. That's not a criticism, it's an observation. It's not bad. It's natural. It's normal. It's rational. It's human. Your survival instincts have kicked in. You have disengaged to some extent to preserve the little energy you have, so you can focus on what matters most and recovering.

Nobody is 100% engaged at anything all the time. Parents often object. Some will try to make the case that they are 100% engaged as a parent all the time. It's not true, even for the best parents.

Some days they may be 100% engaged. "Okay, kids," they announce, "today is going to be the best day of your life. We're going to do this, and this, and this, and this, and this, and this . . . and then we're going to have lunch."

But on other days, these same parents are exhausted, sick, depressed, preoccupied with a crisis, or distracted by some other aspect of their lives. On these days, they say to their children, "Go outside and play, kids." It's a different level of engagement. It doesn't make them bad parents. It happens to all parents. It's natural. It's normal. It's rational. It's human. Parents are constantly engaging and disengaging.

"I have come so that you may have life and have it to the fullest," was Jesus' promise. (John 10:10) Life to the fullest is a highly engaged life.

Now you may be thinking, "I am not living a very engaged life." That's okay. Learning to listen to the three ordinary voices of God is going to change that. You may be thinking, "I'm only about 50% engaged in my marriage." "I'm only about 30% engaged in my personal finances." "I'm about 65% engaged in my spiritual life." That's okay. Knowing where we are helps us to plot a path to where God is calling us to be.

Piercing clarity and massive engagement are just two of the vast benefits that flow to us when we listen to God.

It doesn't matter what level of engagement or disengagement you are experiencing in any aspect of your life, it's time to talk to God about each area of your life and time to listen to what he has to say about the best way to proceed.

But along the way, remember to watch out for these three things we discussed. When I am striving earnestly to listen to the voice of God, I get focused, energized, and invigorated.

Focused. Energized. Invigorated.

And let me share something else I have observed. Any time I am not focused, energized, and invigorated, that's a reliable indicator that I am not listening to the voice of God, or worse, that I am ignoring his voice and actively pursuing my own selfish plans and desires.

Personal clarity leads to massive engagement leads to focused, energized, and invigorated. These are the fruits of listening to the three ordinary voices of God.

WILL YOU LISTEN?

One of the fastest ways to improve any relationship is to become a better listener. Most people assume they are good at listening to those they love, but research suggests we may be overestimating our efforts.

96% of people believe they are good listeners, and yet, we retain only about 50% of what others say. Think about that for a moment. How long have you been married? Thirty years? Your spouse only heard half of what you said. No wonder we feel misunderstood and have disagreements.

And our confidence that we are good listeners makes us even worse at listening, because it prevents us from approaching listening with focused intention.

Learning to listen is an art.

It's easy to question whether God speaks to us, but the preponderance of evidence suggests we should give our attention to another question. This more pertinent question, the question that confronts us daily is: Will you listen? And the question that follows next is: Will you carry out what God asks of you?

The first step is learning to listen. Not only learning to listen to God, but learning to listen in general—to everyone in your life. Thomas Aquinas taught, "Grace builds on nature." So, before we learn to listen to supernatural voices, we need first to listen to the ordinary voices we hear every day.

When we learn to listen, we acquire a quintessential life skill. The older I get the more I realize how vital listening is to vibrant relationships. It is also the most efficient way to improve any relationship—especially our relationship with God.

As you become a better listener, your relationships will improve—guaranteed! Not hopefully, or maybe. Definitely. And I'll let you in on two secrets: Most people don't have one person they feel listens to them deeply, and everybody loves a good listener.

Here are twelve ways to become a better listener:

1. Find the right setting for the conversation.

2. Face the speaker and maintain regular eye contact.

3. Let go of your agenda.

4. Don't interrupt.

5. Listen without judging.

6. Don't try to guess what the other person is going to say.

7. Resist the temptation to reach a conclusion before the person is finished.

8. Don't start planning what to say next while the other person is still speaking.

9. Don't impose your opinions.

10. Listen to the whole person by being aware of non-verbal cues.

11. Stay focused.

12. Ask questions.

The world is full of people who feel misunderstood, unloved, and unheard. So much of this pain and suffering could be alleviated if we would each just slow down and do a little more selfless listening.

We don't teach people how to become great listeners. That's sad. But it is tragic that we don't teach people how to listen to God.

And why aren't we better listeners? Is it because we are so busy? That's one reason, but not the main reason. We are busy, but when we do sit down for a few minutes with those we love, why do we hear so little of what the other person is trying to convey? It's because we are so self-focused.

Listening is an activity centered on others. But most of the time when we are "listening" we are thinking about what we want to say next or judging how what the other person is saying affects us. This is self-focused listening that all but guarantees we will not hear what the other person is trying to convey.

The piercing truth is that listening is a state of humility. Humility is the essence of listening. And humility is in short supply in our culture. We live in a culture where everyone wants to talk, and nobody wants to listen. We shouldn't be surprised that so many people feel misunderstood. We shouldn't be surprised that there is so much division.

Listening well is a state of heightened humility marked by setting aside one's personal preferences and agendas.

Learning to listen to the voice of God and having the courage to follow where he leads are two different matters, but beautifully connected.

We could ask the question in this way: Will you be obedient to what you hear?

Obedience is one of the least popular words in our culture today. We understand obedience as carrying out the commands of a superior, submitting to the orders of a leader, or following someone else's direction. But the word obedience comes from the Latin verb *obedire*, which means, "to listen deeply."

Most people do not seek wise counsel. Most people are not coachable. Most people are destroying themselves a little more with every choice they make. Most people aren't interested in the will of God. Are you willing to be different?

When we listen deeply, we understand more completely the reasons we are being directed to do something, and the more we understand, the easier it will be to carry out what is being asked of us.

Obedience requires us to set down our personal preferences and desires. Obedience goes beyond the normal humility of listening. But in our self-obsessed society, most people want to do whatever they want, whenever they want, and many can't be convinced to listen to reason (never mind wisdom).

Our desire to do what we want, when we want, with whom we want, is strong. But it is not insurmountable. It can be tamed, but first it must be observed and acknowledged in order to begin to overcome it.

Listening to God is an act of hopeful expectation.

Listening to God requires an open heart.

Listening to God requires us to set aside our personal preferences and agendas.

Listening to God involves letting go of our stubborn and prideful desire to do whatever we want.

Listening to God requires humility.

Listening to God is an act of surrender.

Will you listen? That's the only variable. God *has been* speaking to you, he *is* speaking to you, and he will *continue* to speak to you. Will you listen? And how will you listen? Do you remember a time in your life when you really wanted to hear what someone had to say? Do you remember being in love and listening closely to every word your beloved spoke, mumbled, whispered? Will you listen to God like that? Will you listen eagerly or begrudgingly? Will you listen with childlike curiosity or jaded skepticism?

Open your heart and listen to the voice of God and you will find yourself on the verge of all new things.

CHAPTER TWO:
THE FIRST VOICE: NEEDS

EVERY PARENT'S DREAM

Some parents want their children to become doctors and lawyers, others want their kids to play baseball or football, but every parent wants their child to make good decisions. They wonder during the day and stay awake at night, hoping their children will choose wisely.

This is no coincidence because it was God's dream for all his children first. God wants you to become a phenomenal decision maker. And this is one of the most practical reasons to listen to the voice of God. Few things will improve your life more than becoming a great decision maker.

Those of you who are parents, ask yourself: How happy would you be if someone could guarantee you that your children would make great decisions? How happy are you when you see your child make a great decision?

You want your child to become a phenomenal decision maker. You didn't come up with that on your own as a parent. You plagiarized from God.

You are God's child, and he has the same dream for you. God wants you to become a phenomenal decision maker. How are you doing? Are you a good decision maker? How good? If you had to rate yourself between one and ten, how would you score yourself as a decision maker? Do you have a proven process you use for making decisions?

And while you're thinking about that, how good are you at saying no? Do you find it easy to say no when someone asks you to do something, but you are already overcommitted? Or do you find yourself saying yes to things all the time and wondering later why you did?

And one more way to think about it: Are you a decisive person?

Most people are not decisive, they find it excruciatingly difficult to say no, and they are poor decision makers.

We make horrible decisions: big ones, small ones, and medium-size horrible decisions too. Why? It's not because we are stupid or incapable of making good choices. It's because we don't live in the wisdom we have already acquired. Once we wander away from that wisdom, we get stuck in the quicksand of selfishness and the fear of missing out. The other reason we make poor choices is because we don't engage God in the conversation. Once we exclude our principal advisor and wisest counselor, it's too easy to get dragged down by the quagmire of everyone else's feelings. And once we start making decisions based on our feelings or other people's feelings, we are without a doubt the man who built his house on sand. This is where you start to feel guilty about saying no to something any rational person would tell you to say no to. This is where you obsess about turning down an invitation, and offending someone who, depending on the day, may or may not notice if you are there. This is when we fall into the black hole of wanting everyone to like us and become addicted to external validation. And once we start making decisions based on getting people to like us, we have joined Dante and Virgil on their tour of Purgatory.

And still, God's dream remains. He wants you to become a phenomenal decision maker.

Live your life for an audience of one. There is only one opinion that matters: God's. Seek his will in all things, and once you have a sense of what his will is, execute it with passion and purpose. The piece between the seeking and the executing is what this book is about. That's the part where we listen to the voice of God.

If we don't, we will almost certainly find ourselves saying yes to things we should say no to, and no to things we should be saying yes to.

And with every poor decision the chaos and confusion of our lives will escalate.

Add to this whirlwind one of this century's most popular pieces of culture trash and you have a perfect storm that all but guarantees few wise decisions will be made. I am referring to FOMO—Fear of Missing Out.

We should be afraid of missing out, but not in the way most people think. When people say they are afraid of missing out, they are afraid of missing out on everything. This of course is ridiculous, bordering on insane, because the unavoidable and indisputable reality of life is that we miss out on almost everything.

What should you be afraid of missing out on? The one path God imagined for you from the beginning of time. This is a righteous fear. It's an enlightened fear that will keep you from wasting whatever is left of your one short life.

Do you ever look at someone else's life, observe that it has gone horribly wrong, and wonder how it happened?

Let me tell you a story. I've got a friend and for the sake of privacy let's say his name is Paul. A few weeks ago, I called Paul and this was our conversation.

"Paul, I'm glad I got ahold of you. How are you?"

"Good," Paul replied.

"How's work?" I asked.

"Good," Paul replied.

"How is Julie?" (Julie is Paul's girlfriend).

"She's great. Just got a fabulous promotion at work."

"Is she the one for you, Paul?"

"No," he replied. He said it casually but firmly. He said it without hesitation. I could tell he'd thought about it. Julie is not the one for Paul, and Paul knows it.

"You didn't take too long to think about that," I commented.

"I know. I've been thinking about it. She's great. Better than great, and I really like her. But she's just not the one for me."

They have been dating for three years, so I was surprised by this revelation, and I said, "Well I'm sorry to hear that. When are you planning to tell her and break up?"

"Oh no," Paul said, "We're not breaking up. What gave you that idea?"

Baffled, I mirrored back to him what I thought I had just heard and why I had come to what I thought was an obvious conclusion: "Let me make sure I've got this right, Paul. You're dating Julie, you've been dating Julie for three years, and you really like her. You know she's not the one for you, but you're not breaking up with her because you really like her."

He said, "Yep," again in a way so casual that it sounded like the only logical conclusion. Only it wasn't.

So, I asked him, "What are you doing Friday night?"

"Friday night I'm taking Julie to see that new movie."

Here's the problem. On Friday night, when Paul was at that movie with Julie, that might've been the night he was going to meet the woman God created just for him.

When we say yes to stuff that we know isn't for us, we miss out on the stuff that God created just for us.

Think on that. The stakes are high. Much higher than most people ever consider. When you say yes to things that you know are not for you, you miss out on all the people, things, and experiences that God created just for you. And that's the stuff we're yearning for, that's the stuff that sends a chill up your back, that's the stuff worth chasing.

God wants your yes to be a passionate yes, and he wants your no to be a resolute no. God wants you to become a phenomenal decision maker. And that is one of the many reasons we need to learn how to listen to his voice in our lives—at key moments, but also in the hustle and bustle of everyday life.

There are many reasons to acquire the skill of listening to God, but few are more practical than how it will raise the quality of decisions you make.

THE FIRST VOICE: THE BASICS

To be human is to need. This has perhaps never been more eloquently expressed than by Saint Paul in his speech to the Athenians, "For it is in him that we live, and move, and have our being." (Acts 17:28) This beautiful passage presents the proximity of God. He is not a distant and anonymous God, but near and present. It also demonstrates our complete and utter reliance on him.

We are quick to forget our immense need. We are quick to forget our total dependance on God. We are quick to forget God in general, but if God forgot us for even a nanosecond we would cease to exist.

"In him we live, and move, and have our being." This is the very definition of need, but we forget how needy we are.

The first ordinary voice of God is: need.

If you don't eat, you will die. It may take a few days, but if you don't eat you will soon die. You have a legitimate need for food. Who gave you that need? If you don't breathe, you will die even faster. You have a legitimate need for air to breathe. Who gave you that need? If you don't sleep, you will go crazy. Literally insane. Who gave you that need? These are the simplest ways to understand that we all have legitimate needs.

God gave us these needs and he speaks to you through your needs. Why do you think he made us this way? Clues. Clues about what? How to live life to the fullest. How to be happy. How to live the abundant life that Jesus describes in the Gospel.

You are wonderfully made. You were created on purpose and for a purpose. And your needs are one of the powerful ways that God speaks to you every day. Your needs brilliantly lead you toward your unique mission and the best way to live. (As do your talents and truest desires, which we will discover in the next two chapters).

God created us purposefully and mercifully with needs. Your needs are the voice of God speaking to you in a beautiful, practical, ordinary way.

THE FOUR ASPECTS OF THE HUMAN PERSON

The best way to explore the scope of our needs is through the four aspects of the human person: physical, emotional, intellectual, and spiritual. You have legitimate needs in all four areas. God created you with these needs, and as such, they provide clues about who you are and how to live your one short life.

Our culture is obsessed with the second and third ordinary voices—talent and desire—but as you will soon discover, your overall happiness is much more dependent on listening to the first voice: need.

You have physical, emotional, intellectual, and spiritual needs, and God gave them to you as a map to happiness, and so much more. If you learn to listen to your needs, you will find yourself on the threshold of human flourishing.

But before we get too deep into the subject, I feel compelled to make it clear that most of us are very confused about what our legitimate needs are. This is the result of massive cultural confusion about the difference between *needs* and *wants*. And it is right here that it becomes disturbingly easy to begin to mis-live our one precious life.

So, it might be best to assume at this point that you do not know what your needs are. Open your heart to discovering your true needs for the first time—and to hearing God speak to you through them.

Your Physical Needs

Your physical needs are relatively easy to understand. You have a legitimate need for food, water, shelter, clothing, and exercise. These are some core examples. The primary reason our physical needs are so easily understood is because if we neglect them, the consequences are both considerable and immediate.

Regular exercise, a balanced diet, and regular sleep are three of the easiest ways to increase our passion, energy, and enthusiasm for life. They are among our simplest legitimate needs and contribute massively to the well-being of the whole person. Physical well-being is the foundation upon which we build our lives. This is often forgotten in our quest for other shiny things of less import. But unless we diligently attend to our physical needs, our capacity in all other areas of our life will be reduced.

This body is our home in the physical realm. It is also a temple of the Holy Spirit. I personally find this to be an uncomfortable truth. I have treated my body quite poorly at times. I have my reasons and justifications, but they amount to little more than excuses and self-deceptions. The brutal truth is I have traded my health for pleasure, ambition, and a poor understanding of service to God and others. I have neglected my physical needs by going days without sleep to complete a project or a manuscript. The first time I had cancer I did what my doctors asked but didn't take the message God was sending seriously. I treated it like an inconvenience and pressed on living life at five hundred miles an hour. I have done a poor job of treating my body as a temple of the Holy Spirit. I have work to do in this regard.

What is God saying to you through your physical needs at this time of your life?

Your Emotional Needs

Your emotional needs are more subtle than your physical needs, but they provide an immensely powerful conduit through which to hear

God's voice.

"What are feelings?" I remember my son, Walter, asking when he was a small boy. "Feelings are messengers," I told him.

Your feelings aren't good or bad, they are just messengers. Learning to listen to these messages is a powerful way to increase knowledge of self and improve relationships.

Take fear, for example. Fear is a very useful emotion. God speaks to us through it primarily to keep us safe. God speaks to us through fear when we get too close to a steep fall. Anger is a very useful emotion too. It may be God pointing out an injustice.

Your emotional needs are vast and varied, and they change in different seasons of your life. They include friendship, community, intimacy, and opportunities to love and be loved.

You also have emotional needs that have a psychological dimension, such as your need for acceptance, understanding, connection, security, validation, autonomy, empathy, trust, and encouragement.

And you have emotional needs with a spiritual dimension, such as your need for meaning and purpose.

Our emotional needs are easier to ignore because they are not necessary for immediate survival. The effect of neglecting them may take months or even years to become debilitating. And yet, at every step along the way, neglecting them will diminish our joy and produce decline in other ways that prevent us from flourishing.

Emotional starvation, while not life threatening, does have symptoms. For some of us, emotional starvation can lead to radical mood swings, for others to general lethargy, for others yet, to anger, bitterness, and resentment. The heart suffers and the body cries out. Most of all, emotional starvation leads to distortions in our character and prevents us from becoming the-best-version-of-ourselves.

For most people, their legitimate emotional needs are fulfilled by spending time with family, friends, a spouse, a boyfriend or girlfriend, colleagues, and perhaps a mentor or spiritual director.

One of our dominant emotional needs is our need for acceptance. We all need people in our lives who, through their actions, say, "I see you. I hear you. You matter. I am with you. I care."

We all need to feel we belong. In the face of rejection, we may put on a brave face and pretend that we can survive. It's true. We can *survive* without the nurturing that acceptance provides. But we cannot *thrive* without it.

Acceptance is one of the forces that drives human behavior. Our need to be accepted is powerful, and it is astounding what most people will do to gain some sort of acceptance or sense of belonging.

Peer pressure takes full advantage of this need to be accepted. Under the influence of peer pressure, people do things that they would not do if they were alone (and in many cases would prefer not to do), simply because they do not want to be excluded from a particular social circle. There is perhaps no greater example of our need to belong and feel accepted.

We seek this sense of belonging in hundreds of different ways at work, at school, within our family, in the context of our intimate relationships, and by joining clubs, churches, and committees. Some of the ways we try to have this need met are healthy and help us to pursue our essential purpose. Others are not healthy and can prevent us from flourishing.

We have a great need for acceptance and a sense of belonging.

This makes it easier to understand why people join gangs and cults. Just like you and me, people who join gangs and cults have a legitimate need for acceptance and a sense of belonging. They just don't have the options you and I have.

Our needs are powerful. In many cases, if they are not fulfilled in healthy ways, they will seek their own satisfaction in self-destructive ways.

Now let's explore our emotional need for dynamic friendship. While we certainly need acceptance, we also have a need to be encouraged and challenged to change and grow.

The truth about friendship is this: We learn more from our friends than we ever will from books, and as a result, we become like the people we spend time with.

If your friends only want to watch television, drink beer, eat pizza, and play video games...chances are you will adopt their lifestyle. If your friends work out at the gym four times a week and fill their weekends with outdoor activities...chances are you will adopt their lifestyle.

The friends we choose either raise or lower our standards. We all need people in our lives who raise our standards and challenge us to become the-best-version-of-ourselves.

Our greatest emotional need is for intimacy. Beyond the primary needs for food, water, sleep, and air to breathe, intimacy is the greatest need of the human person. Intimacy is one thing a person cannot live happily without.

Sex is not intimacy. Almost every reference to intimacy in modern popular culture is a reference to sex. The culture thinks sex and intimacy are the same thing. They are not.

Human beings yearn above all else for intimacy. We desire happiness, and sometimes we confuse this desire for happiness with a desire for pleasure and possessions. But once we have experienced the pleasure or attained the possessions, we are still left wanting. Wanting what? Intimacy. Our desire for happiness is ultimately a desire for intimacy. If we have intimacy, we can go without an awful lot and still be happy. Without intimacy, all the riches of the world cannot satisfy our hungry hearts. Until we experience intimacy, our hearts remain restless, irritable, and discontented.

So, what is intimacy? Intimacy is mutual self-revelation.

Life is a journey of self-discovery and self-revelation. Every day, in a thousand ways, we discover ourselves in new ways and reveal ourselves to the people around us. Everything we say and do reveals something about who we are and what we value. Even the things we don't say and the things we don't do tell others something about us. Life is about sharing ourselves with humanity at this moment in history.

Relationships are also a process of self-revelation. But far too often we spend our time and energy hiding our true selves from each other in relationships. This is where we encounter the great paradox that surrounds our struggle for intimacy. The entire human experience is a quest for harmony amid opposing forces, and our quest for intimacy is no different.

We want intimacy. We need intimacy. But we are afraid. We are desperately afraid that if people really knew us, they wouldn't love us. As a result, our fear of rejection and our need for intimacy are constantly at odds with each other.

Intimacy requires that we allow another person to discover what moves us, what inspires us, what drives us, what eats away at us, what we are running toward, what we are running from, what silent self-destructive enemies lie within us, and what wild and wonderful dreams we hold in our hearts.

To be truly intimate with another person is to share every aspect of yourself with that person. We have to be willing to take off our masks and let down our guard, to set aside our pretenses and to share what is shaping us and directing our lives. This is the greatest gift we can give to another human being: to allow him or her to simply see us for who we are, with our strengths and weaknesses, faults, failings, flaws, defects, talents, abilities, achievements, and potential.

Intimacy requires that we allow another person into our heart, mind, body, and soul. In its purest form, it is a complete and unrestrained sharing of self. Not all relationships are worthy of such a complete intimacy, but our primary relationship should be.

What is intimacy? It is the process of mutual self-revelation that inspires us to give ourselves completely to another person in the mystery we call love.

Relationships expand in direct proportion to our ability to reveal ourselves to the other person. Yet most people spend their lives hiding their true selves and pretending they are somebody that they are not.

There are ways to set people at ease so they feel comfortable engaging in the self-revelation that is intimacy. And to this end, there are important questions for us all to consider: Do we provide a non-judgmental environment for others to reveal themselves to us? Do we affirm those we love by complimenting them and expressing gratitude, not only for what they do, but for who they are? When others make mistakes, are we quick to judge, ridicule, and gossip, or do we acknowledge it as a learning experience and part of their journey? Are we willing to take the first step, making ourselves vulnerable, and revealing our true selves to others?

Nothing satisfies the human person like intimacy. Create an environment where people feel safe to be themselves and reveal themselves, and together you will drink from the springs of intimacy.

We live in the age of hyper-communication. The communication revolution has made it easier than ever before to communicate and has transformed the way we live. And yet, it hasn't increased our ability or willingness to communicate in meaningful ways. Our communication is shallower and more superficial than ever before.

The reason we neglect most of our legitimate needs is that they require our rarest resources: time and energy. Relationships are no different.

Relationships thrive under one condition: carefree timelessness. What is carefree timelessness? It is time together without an agenda.

Quality time is now the discredited fantasy of an age that wanted more of everything except the things that really mattered. You cannot schedule quality time with your spouse or with your children. If you want twenty minutes of quality time with someone, schedule three or four hours with them one afternoon, and chances are, somewhere in the middle of that three or four hours you will have your twenty minutes of quality time.

We live busy lives in a busy world. All this busyness is not conducive to dynamic relationships. And it is time we were honest about that. Too often the time we do set aside for relationships is on the perimeters of our already busy lives, so we approach our relationships without the energy they demand in order to be fruitful and fulfilling.

Relationships don't thrive under the pressures of our hectic schedules. All of life's important relationships thrive under the condition of carefree timelessness. We will either gift our relationships with this type of time or not, but without carefree timelessness our ability to get to know each other is virtually non-existent and the chances of a relationship thriving plummet.

How is God speaking to you through your emotional needs at this time of your life?

Your Intellectual Needs

Your intellectual needs are perhaps the easiest to ignore. You have a legitimate need to feed your mind, explore your curiosity, expand your knowledge, and sharpen your intellectual abilities.

Ideas shape our lives. Ideas shape history. We all have a need for a constant flow of ideas that inspire us, challenge us, illumine our minds, teach us about ourselves and our world, show us what is possible, and encourage us to become all God created us to be.

We need a diet of the mind just as much as we need a diet of the body. The ideas we feed our mind today tend to form our lives tomorrow.

Think of it in this way: We become the stories we listen to. It doesn't matter if we get those stories from movies, music, television, newspapers, magazines, videogames, social media, politicians, friends, or books—the stories we listen to form our lives.

If you want to understand any period in history, simply ask two questions: Who were the storytellers? And what story were they telling?

History is full of storytellers. But the quality and significance of their stories vary greatly. Winston Churchill, Francis of Assisi, Charlemagne, Napoleon, Charlie Chaplin, Adolf Hitler, Bob Dylan, Mother Teresa, Mahatma Gandhi, Abraham Lincoln, Marilyn Monroe, Nelson Mandela, and Jesus each told a story.

If you want to know how a nation will be different tomorrow from the way it was yesterday, find out how the stories that nation is listening to are different from the stories of yesterday. If you discover that the stories we are listening to have less meaning, contain more violence, and rather than inspiring us and raising our standards, they appeal more and more to the lowest common denominator, you can be sure that in the future our lives will have less meaning, contain more violence, and be more focused on the lowest common denominator.

We become the stories we listen to. What stories are you listening to? Who are the central storytellers in your life? What stories are you allowing to form who you are becoming and the life you are living?

Our intellectual needs are never urgent, so it is easy to overlook them. When was the last time you said to yourself, "I urgently need to read a good book today"? It doesn't happen. Why? For one, our intellectual needs are not primary needs. If we neglect them, we won't die. But mental vitality leads to physical, emotional, and spiritual vitality. Everything in our lives begins as a thought.

The reason people neglect their intellectual development is that they associate books and learning with school and work. Most people have very little leisure time, and they don't want to spend that time doing what they perceive as "work." One of the great tragedies of modern education systems is that they are failing to instill a love of learning. All too often, learning is seen only as a means to an end. It is necessary to pass an exam, or get a degree, or gain a promotion. Learning, like so many other aspects of modern living, has been violently disconnected from our essential purpose.

Some may argue that intellectually we are more advanced than ever before. This is certainly true, but the nature of our knowledge has become increasingly more specialized. The trend is for our professional knowledge, and in many cases, training, to become more and more specific. A narrower base of knowledge necessarily creates a narrower worldview.

Add to all these factors the fact that most people feel exhausted by the intellectual demands being made upon them in the workplace, and it is easy to understand why a large proportion of people like to dump themselves in front of the television for hours each evening after work.

When we take all of this into account, it is easy to understand why most people neglect their legitimate need for personal intellectual stimulation.

At the same time, to neglect our phenomenal abilities to think, reason, decide, imagine, and dream is to enormously limit our potential.

We all have intellectual needs. Our intellectual needs may vary significantly from person to person, and while many are involved in intellectually engaging occupations, we all need other types of intellectual stimulation. In fact, the greater our professional intellectual stimulation, the greater need we have for other forms of intellectual nourishment to create a balance. Besides, it is highly unlikely that our professional intellectual efforts suit our individual needs at each time and place in life's journey.

In the category of personal intellectual stimulation, we could read magazines about fashion, gardening, sports, finance, music, or any other area of interest. We will be entertained, but it is unlikely that we will be challenged to raise our standards and become the-best-version-of-ourselves. To really stretch ourselves, we must delve into the wisdom writings. Selections could include a variety of philosophical texts, the writings of countless spiritual leaders past and present, and the Scriptures. It is in these writings that the intellect comes face-to-face with the most profound questions and truths about the world, creation, God, humanity, and our individual journeys.

Our intellectual needs are also many and varied. Most of us have need for a professional intellectual focus. We all need different forms of entertaining intellectual stimulation. But it's important to challenge ourselves to move beyond these intellectual comfort zones and to embrace writings that challenge us to ponder the deeper questions, truths, and mysteries of our existence. As Mark Twain observed, "The man who does not read good books has no advantage over the man who cannot read them."

Books change our lives. I believe that with my whole heart. I like to ask people about the greatest period of transformation in their lives. They tell me it was five years ago or seven years ago, they tell me it was when they got cancer or lost their job, they tell me it was in the town they grew up in or in a city where they didn't know anyone. "What were you reading at the time?" I like to ask them next. Nine out of ten times, their eyes light up and they say, "I was reading... and that book changed my life."

I have several thousand books. But on one shelf of one of the two bookcases in my study where I write, at eye level, I have thirty-seven books. Each of those books has had an enormous impact on my life. I can tell you where I bought them, what city of the world I was in when I read them, and what the circumstances and situations of my life were at the time. There are books about philosophy, theology, psychology, business, personal development, and history. There are some incredible novels and biographies, and there on that shelf you will find some of the greatest spiritual and inspirational classics of all time. It is, in a sense, my own Great Books collection.

From time to time, when I become discouraged, confused, lonely, fearful, or simply begin to doubt my life and myself, I go to that bookshelf. I glance along that row of books, and one of those books calls out to me. I take it from the shelf and rediscover the inspiration that first earned it a place on the top shelf.

Our bodies need regular exercise and a balanced diet, and so do our minds. You have a legitimate need to nourish your mind. If you choose the right diet of the mind, your life will be directed by ideas of excellence and greatness. If you allow the media and secular culture to select your intellectual diet, your life will be formed by distraction and mediocrity.

Books change our lives. Begin your own collection of great books.

Choose books that will help you to achieve your essential purpose and become the-best-version-of-yourself. Make daily reading one of the defining habits of your life.

You have intellectual needs. God gave them to you and he speaks to you through them. What is God saying to you through your intellectual needs at this time of your life?

Your Spiritual Needs

Your spiritual needs are for stillness, silence, solitude, simplicity, Scriptures, and Sacraments. Even though your spiritual needs are astoundingly important, they are easily ignored, and the results of doing so appear not to be impactful until long after we first start ignoring them. But the negative impact on our ability to thrive is massive and immediate.

Only here in the area of spirituality do we come to fully understand our other legitimate needs—physical, emotional, and intellectual—and gain the insight to live a life that enriches, upholds, and protects our well-being in each of these areas.

Silence

The noise of the world is preventing us from hearing the gentle voice within that always counsels us to embrace the-best-version-of-ourselves. We will begin to hear this voice again only when we make a habit of withdrawing from the noise of the world and immersing ourselves in silence. We needn't spend hours in silence each day, but nothing brings priority to our days like a period of silence each morning.

Everyday life poses questions. We all have a need to search our hearts for answers to those questions. Every day we are faced with a myriad of choices and opportunities. We need time away from all the other voices to discern which of these choices and opportunities will enable us to become the-best-version-of-ourselves and which are merely distractions. It has been my experience that these exercises are performed most effectively alone, in the precious solitude of the classroom of silence.

It is also in silence and solitude that life's preeminent challenge is proposed to us. Brother Silence and Sister Solitude unveil the person we are today with all our strengths and weaknesses, but they also remind us of the better person we know we can be.

In the silence, we see at one time the person we are now and the person we are capable of becoming. Seeing these two visions at one time automatically challenges us to change and grow. It is precisely for this reason that we fill our lives with noise, to distract ourselves from the challenge to change.

Silence has been a great friend to the extraordinary men and women of every age. Many of life's great lessons can be learned only in the classroom of silence, especially those that teach us about our individual talents and how we can use them to fulfill our destiny.

The wisest people of every culture under the sun have sought the counsel of silence for millennia.

Pythagoras, the Greek philosopher and mathematician (580–500 BC) wrote: "Learn to be silent. Let your quiet mind listen and absorb."

Writing about the importance of silence and solitude, Blaise Pascal, the seventeenth-century French philosopher, scientist, mathematician, and writer, wrote: "All of man's miseries derive from not being able to sit quietly in a room alone."

Franz Kafka, the Czech novelist, philosopher, and poet, wrote: "You need not leave your room. Remain sitting at your table and listen. You need not even listen, simply wait. You need not even wait, just learn to become quiet, and still and solitary. The world will freely offer itself to you to be unmasked. It has no choice; it will roll in ecstasy at your feet."

Learn to be quiet. Learn to be still. In this silence God always speaks.

Simplicity

We come now to the spiritual need of simplicity. Simplicity is one of the governing principles of the universe, yet with every passing century, humanity looks to greater complexity to solve its problems and improve its life.

Who among us needs a little more complexity in their lives? None of us! What our lives desperately need is the liberation of simplicity.

If we learn once again to listen to the gentle voice within, we will hear it counseling us many times a day to simplify our lives. When the voices of the world propose the multiple complexities of modern living, the gentle voice within will whisper: Why complicate your life? Over time we will learn to turn our backs on a multitude of opportunities in order to preserve the peace in our hearts that is born from the blessed simplicity that the world despises.

Simplify. Simplify. Simplify your life and you will find the inner peace that the poets and saints of every age have coveted more than any possession.

Silence. Solitude. Simplicity. Three great friends! They may be the subtlest of our legitimate needs, but when they are honored, our spirits soar to unimaginable heights, and we are left only to wonder how or why we ever followed the promptings of all the jeering voices of this world.

The Scriptures

Stillness, silence, solitude, and simplicity are all disciplines that allow us to fully participate and benefit from the Scriptures and the Sacraments.

If the Bible is the inspired Word of God, why do you think so few people read it regularly and study it attentively? Because it has the power to transform our lives. Seriously. That's not a typo.

God wants to transform you and your life. Too often when we pray, we pray for tweaking. We want God to tweak some aspect of our lives. But God isn't interested in tweaking. God isn't in the business of tweaking; God is in the business of transformation. He wants to turn your life upside down, which, as it turns out, is right side up. He wants to transform the way you think about yourself, he wants to transform the way you think about relationships, he wants to transform the way you think about money and career, and he wants to transform the way you think about the world and the culture.

If you want to see something incredible, personal miracles, start reading one chapter of the Bible each day and praying for transformation. Start with the New Testament. Ask God to transform you and your life. Pray for transformation. Most people have never prayed a prayer of transformation.

Let's pray one together, right now:

Loving Father, I invite you into my life today and make myself available to you. Help me to become the-best-version-of-myself by seeking your will and becoming a living example of your love in the world. Open my heart to the areas of my life that need to change in order for me to carry out the mission and experience the joy you have imagined for my life. Inspire me to live the Catholic faith in ways that are dynamic and engaging. Show me how to best get involved in the life of my parish. Make our community hungry for best practices and continuous learning. Give me courage when I am afraid, hope when I am discouraged, and clarity in times of decision. Teach me to enjoy uncertainty and lead your Church to become all you imagined it would be for the people of our times. Amen.

The truth is, your happiness depends upon discovering God's will for your life, and the Bible is an invaluable gift for discerning God's will. The Scriptures are one of God's most direct ways of speaking into our lives. But too often we are not interested in discovering the will of God. Usually we are more interested in "my will be done" than "Thy will be done." Think about it: When was the last time you actively sought out

God's will in a situation?

The Bible helps lead us to God's mysterious and fabulous plan for our lives—and that is always transformational. This is not just another book. If you have never truly encountered Jesus in the Scriptures now is your time.

The Sacraments

Jesus gave us the Sacraments to feed our souls and transform us spiritually. All seven are deeply rooted in the Scriptures, and through them, we receive the grace necessary to live the way God invites us to live—with generosity and kindness, with patience and humility, and with a love that sets us apart.

The Sacraments are the center of the life of the Church. And while the Sacraments are surrounded by profound rituals, it's important not to forget what they are at their core: an encounter with Jesus Christ.

It is hard to overstate the vital role of the Sacraments in our walk with God. *The Catechism of the Catholic Church* notes that, "The seven sacraments touch all the stages and all the important moments of Christian life: they give birth and increase, healing and mission to the Christian's life of faith. There is thus a certain resemblance between the stages of natural life and the stages of the spiritual life." (CCC 1210)

In a sense, the Sacraments are God's systematic plan to provide for all our spiritual needs. In Baptism, he adopts us and gives us an eternal family. In Reconciliation, he offers the balm of forgiveness. In the Eucharist, he nourishes our souls and invites us into deep silence and stillness. In Confirmation, he empowers us for mission and a life of purpose. In Anointing of the Sick, he offers healing, both physical and spiritual, in moments of trial. In Marriage, he unites man and woman in a bond of inseparable love and self-revelation. In Holy Orders, he calls specific men to a life of service and sacrifice.

Since you are reading this book, and you have gotten this far, I feel safe making the assumption that you genuinely desire to hear God's voice in your life. If that is the case, how foolish would it be not to embrace the inspired word of God in the Scriptures and the encounters with Jesus offered in each of the Sacraments?

The Sacraments are a profound source of unlimited grace, they pour incredible grace into our lives in a direct and powerful way. Embrace them with a new and radical urgency. Accept these divine gifts. Cherish them.

When we attend to our legitimate spiritual needs, everything else seems to fall into perspective. Only then are we able to let go of the past, wait patiently for the future, and live with an intense passion for life in the joy of the here and now. We feel healthy. We feel more fully alive. Our lives fill with vitality, and life becomes an exciting adventure instead of the day-to-day drudgery of counting the minutes away.

The fulfillment of our legitimate spiritual needs leads us to place our essential purpose at the center of our daily lives. When silence, solitude, and simplicity become a part of the fabric of our lives, we are much less inclined to neglect our other legitimate needs. Only with the focus, perspective, and vitality that are born from the spiritual disciplines will we ever learn to transform each moment and experience of our lives into opportunities to become the-best-version-of-ourselves. Spirituality brings clarity, direction, continuity, and integrity to our lives.

How have you been tending to your spiritual needs? How have you been neglecting your spiritual needs? How do you think God is speaking to you through your spiritual needs during this season of your life?

When you look at the four aspects of the human person (physical, emotional, intellectual, spiritual) it becomes clear: We all have needs. We need air to breathe, water to drink, and food to eat. We need to love and be loved. We need to accept and appreciate others and to be accepted and appreciated by others. We need to learn, to change, and to grow. We need to remember who we truly are and what matters most. We *need*.

This is how God made us as human beings. He's given us our legitimate needs as a map to happiness. That is astoundingly clear. The question becomes: What prevents us from embracing the happiness we were made for?

THE HAPPINESS PARADOX

We pretend that human happiness is a vast mystery. It isn't. We pretend to be baffled by the process that leads to happiness. It isn't baffling at all. We complicate the quest for happiness like we do most things. The problem is we have confused ourselves about what we believe will make us happy. What represents happiness to you?

The human heart is on a quest for happiness. Everybody wants to be happy. You want to be happy, and I want to be happy. The human person has a natural thirst for happiness, and we do the things we do because we believe they will make us happy.

From time to time, people do stupid things. We may look at them, scratch our heads, and wonder, "Why would anybody do something so stupid?" Or we may think, "Don't they know that is going to make them miserable?" The fascinating thing is this: The reason people do stupid things is because they mistakenly believe those stupid things will make them happy.

People don't wake up in the morning and ask themselves, "How can I make myself miserable today?" We do the things we do believing they will make us happy.

This is the great modern paradox: We know the things that make us happy; we just don't do them.

Let's consider this also in the context of the four aspects of the human person: physical, emotional, intellectual, and spiritual.

Physically, when you exercise regularly, sleep regularly, eat the right sorts of foods, and balance your diet, how do you feel? You feel fantastic. You feel more fully alive. You're healthier, happier, and you have a richer, more abundant experience of life.

Emotionally, when you give focus and priority to your relationships, what happens? You switch the focus off yourself and onto others. As you do, your ability to love increases. . .and as your ability to love increases, your ability to be loved increases. You become more aware of yourself, develop a more balanced view of life, and experience a deeper sense of fulfillment. You're healthier. You're happier.

Intellectually, when you take ten or fifteen minutes a day to read a good book, what happens? Your vision of yourself expands; your vision of the world expands. You become more focused, more alert, and more vibrant. Clarity replaces confusion. You feel more fully alive, and you are happier.

Finally, spiritually, when you take a few moments each day to step into the classroom of silence and reconnect with yourself and with your God, what happens? The gentle voice within grows stronger, and you develop a deeper sense of peace, purpose, and direction. You're healthier, you're happier, and you have a richer experience of life.

Physically, emotionally, intellectually, and spiritually, we know the things that infuse our lives with passion and enthusiasm. We know the things that make us happy. We just don't do them.

It doesn't make sense, and that is the happiness paradox.

You have needs. To need is to be human. Knowing your needs intimately is essential to human flourishing. You thrive when a good cross-section of your needs are being met. That's when you're most fully alive. That's when joy explodes in your soul.

But it's important to note the phrase "a good cross-section." We are not talking about having all of our needs met at all times. That's not realistic. There is only one place where all your needs can be met and fulfilled, and there is only one person who can meet and fulfill all your needs. God in heaven. This is a critical point in our discussion. Nobody can have all their needs met completely in this messy, imperfect world. And if we try, we will become intolerably selfish, constantly obsessing over our unmet needs. And nothing will make you more miserable than obsessing over yourself. The more I think about myself, the unhappier I become. You will find the same is true for you, I suspect.

We know the things that make us happy. They are simple and few. Now, let's seek to understand why we overlook them.

GETTING WHAT YOU WANT DOESN'T MAKE YOU HAPPY

The reason we overlook the simple things that genuinely make us happy is we get so easily distracted and mesmerized by shiny things. And then we chase these shiny things of little value and less substance.

We live in a culture that isn't interested in needs. We live in a culture obsessed with wants. We neglect our needs because the culture boldly and confidently proclaims, "The meaning of life is to get what you want, and the more you get what you want the happier you'll be."

We yearn for meaning and crave happiness, so we fall into this deception with disturbing ease. Even though we each know, in our own way from personal experience, that it isn't true.

Getting what you want doesn't make you happy. You know that. How do I know that you know? You have tested this theory many times. We all have.

You have wanted things in your life with feverish desire. You have obsessed over the object of your desire. You don't always get what you want, but there have been enough instances when you did get what you wanted for you to know that getting what you want doesn't make you happy.

Perhaps it was a bicycle when you were a child or a car as an adult. Maybe it was a deal, the dream job, the project, the house, the girl, the guy, the handbag, the watch, or the vacation. Whatever it was, it didn't work. It may have provided delightful distraction and momentary pleasure, but it didn't bring you lasting happiness. Whatever it did bring you faded in time, and you moved the focus of your wanting onto something else.

There's a reason it didn't work. You were marvelously created so that trivial things wouldn't satisfy you. Imagine if a trip to the shopping mall could absolutely and completely satisfy you. That would be pretty sad, right? Why? Because it would mean that you were made for nothing more than a trip to the shopping mall. The fading satisfaction of these things is proof that you were made for more. The fading satisfaction provides clues to keep searching.

There have been plenty of times when you have gotten what you wanted, and it didn't bring you the happiness you thought it would. It probably brought you a little happiness for a little while. But that's not what you want. You want lasting happiness in this changing world. So, what did you do? You started chasing something else. Rinse and repeat. Many of us have been making this same mistake, over and over again, our whole lives.

Getting what you want doesn't make you happy. The reason is simple and profound: You simply never can get enough of what you don't really need. It's impossible. Not difficult. Impossible. You can only get enough of what you legitimately need.

To satisfy our desire for happiness it is essential to understand the origins of this desire. Our common desire for happiness isn't coincidence. We were created for happiness.

There is a beautiful passage in *The Catechism of the Catholic Church*. It is the opening lines of Chapter One, and I encourage you to take it to your prayer sometime and meditate deeply on this handful of lines, phrase by phrase, word by word.

"The desire for God is written in the human heart, because man is created by God and for God; and God never ceases to draw man to himself. Only in God will he find the truth and happiness he never stops searching for: The dignity of man rests above all on the fact that he is called to communion with God. This invitation to converse with God is addressed to man as soon as he comes into being. For if man exists it is because God has created him through love, and through love continues to hold him in existence. He cannot live fully according to truth unless he freely acknowledges that love and entrusts himself to his creator." (CCC 27)

We are all searching for truth and happiness. Men and women of all faiths, and those with no faith, all make the same claim. We rush here and there, busying ourselves to the point of misery in search of happiness, but it is only in God that we will find the truth and happiness we never stop searching for.

It is profoundly simple and disturbingly true that most of the world's problems are caused by our confusion over what will make us happy. What do you believe will make you happy? Examine your answer for self-deception. Your motives are a powerful window of self-discovery.

God created you to be reasonably happy in this life and completely happy in the next life. But the culture tells you the path to happiness is getting what you want and that's where most people's lives depart from the path of reasonable happiness and contentment. When we prioritize our wants over what we need, we begin pursuing the wrong things.

Our happiness is more likely to come from fulfilled needs than satisfied wants. But that's doesn't mean needs are good and wants are bad. God gave us both and he speaks to us through both. It just means that needs are primary and wants are secondary.

GOD LOVES ORDER

God loves clarity and order. He is always trying to lead us from chaos to order and from confusion to clarity. Beyond the chaos and confusion that often marks our world, and our lives, we find peace. We speak of peace in the world, but rarely about inner peace. There will be no peace in the world until there is peace in our hearts. The beautiful thing is that you can do something about inner peace. Not next month or next year, but today.

Take a deep breath, close your eyes, and ponder these questions: Is chaos or order reigning inside you today? Are you in a place of clarity or confusion today?

If you are struggling to focus in on the questions, try it this way: Which word best describes your inner life today—chaos or order? Which word best describes how you feel about the direction of your life today—clarity or confusion?

These can be scary questions. But let's consider something even more frightening and tragic: Most people won't even pause to consider these questions. We have neglected the inner life for so long that it seems daunting and overwhelming. So we continue to subscribe to the constant noise, distraction, and activity the culture endlessly serves up.

One glance at their inner life and many people feel ashamed. But if we can step beyond that shame, many of us discover we have never been taught how to establish a vibrant inner life. It's not your fault. But let's start doing something about it today.

If you want to establish a vibrant inner life, defined by clarity and order, God is your best friend in this endeavor. Just let him speak into your life.

The chaos of the world demonstrates how far humanity has wandered away from God. The confusion we often experience making decisions demonstrates how out of touch we are with the voice of God in our own lives.

But God's ready to change that whenever you are.

Let me give you a practical example. You go to church on Sunday. The priest or deacon reads the Gospel. Most people aren't listening. But if you listen, God will speak to you.

You will hear him trying to rearrange your priorities. That's what I hear. You will hear him gently questioning what is at the center of your life. You will hear him challenging you to reconsider how you treat the most important people in your life.

God loves clarity and order, and the peace and joy that come with clarity and order. But the world is full of chaos and confusion. One way to assess the chaos or order in your heart is to consider how you prioritize needs and wants. Needs are primary, wants are secondary. When these get out of order in our hearts, chaos and confusion quickly begin to reign in every area of our lives.

We have established that we have legitimate needs, that these needs are God-given, and that they provide clues about how to live life to the fullest. It's time to adopt this wisdom.

Our priorities have a way of getting discombobulated and misaligned. Are your priorities aligned with worldly success or heavenly glory? Are you living justly, loving tenderly, and walking humbly with your God? Or have you placed yourself at the center of the universe?

If your life is a mad scramble, something is probably way out of alignment. If that's your life, you have a decision to make: Is that how you want to continue to live your life, or are you ready to make a shift?

It may seem overwhelming or even impossible. It isn't. You can make a significant shift, today. How? Start prioritizing your needs rather than your wants.

Start prioritizing your needs rather than your wants. You will be amazed how this simple inner-shift can have an outsized impact on your life.

Wants aren't bad, but they are secondary. It's okay to want things. God gave you the ability to want and our God always acts with purpose. So, if God gave you the ability to want, he gave it to you for a reason. Desire is the third voice, and we will explore that shortly.

Needs are primary, wants are secondary. Keep this essential truth in mind throughout your day as you make decisions, allow it to guide you, and usher the clarity and order God loves into every corner of your life.

GOD WANTS YOU TO SERVE POWERFULLY

"Focusing on your needs is selfish!" Every time I have ever spoken on this topic, someone has come up to me after my presentation to make this argument. Is focusing on our needs selfish? Maybe. That all depends on your answer to this question: Why?

Nobody accuses anybody of being selfish for breathing. Imagine someone said to you, "You're so selfish and annoying. Every time I see you, you're breathing. You do it all the time. Over and over again, incessantly. You're just constantly breathing, breathing, breathing. It's selfish and unchristian."

This is lunacy, right?

Purpose is the key to understanding anything. Why does God want you to attend to your legitimate needs? Does he want you to become completely self-focused, self-interested, self-obsessed? No. God wants you to take care of your legitimate needs for very specific reasons.

The first is this: God wants you to thrive just like any good father would want his children to thrive.

The second reason is this: God wants you to serve powerfully. He wants you to serve powerfully and for a long time, and you cannot do that if you don't attend to your legitimate needs.

There's a reason flight attendants instruct you to put your oxygen mask on first if the plane's cabin loses pressure. It's a simple and beautiful reason: There is no limit to the number of other people you can help once you have your own oxygen mask on. God invites you to attend to your legitimate needs for the same reason.

There is no limit to the number of other people you can serve if you are attending to your own legitimate needs.

What happens if you don't put your oxygen mask on first? You pass out before you can help a single person.

God wants you to serve powerfully. Not like a shooting star, but with the endurance and consistency of the sun.

And this is the third reason: God wants you to serve with joy. It's an ugly thing to serve without joy. We have all seen it and joyless service is ugly.

Joy evaporates from our lives quickly when we neglect our legitimate needs. Try going without sleep for a couple of nights and see how quickly your joy evaporates. It's hard to serve people joyfully when your own needs are not being met.

It's time to relocate your joy. How? By honoring your legitimate needs. You will be amazed how gradually reestablishing your needs as a priority will flood your heart, mind, body, and soul with joy.

God wants you to serve powerfully. He wants you to serve for a long time. And God wants to serve you with joy. You can't do any of this if you don't give your legitimate needs their rightful place in your daily routines and rituals.

The first ordinary voice God uses to speak to us every day of our lives is the voice of need.

CHAPTER THREE:
THE SECOND VOICE: TALENT

THE TWO PATHS

Two paths diverge in every person's life, but it isn't one epic moment of decision like many readers of Robert Frost's poem would like to believe. It's a hundred decisions everyday—what to think, what to say, what to do, who to listen to, who to ignore. There are two paths to choose from in life: To live your life from the inside-out, or to live your life from the outside-in.

The first path—living from the inside-out—leads to inner peace, a strong sense of self based on internal validation, a life of substance, authenticity, an integrated life, continuous growth, clear direction, and a profound sense of purpose and fulfillment.

The other path—living from the outside-in—leads to restlessness, deep personal insecurities based on an unhealthy need for external validation, a superficial life of pretending, wasted potential, a life that lacks direction ruled by distraction and the next shiny thing, a gut-wrenching sense that you are wasting your life, and a profound sense of inadequacy.

There are two paths, and we each get to choose. Not once, but dozens of times every day.

Some of you may be thinking you are too far gone down the second path already. You may be depressed or headed toward despair upon discovering that. Don't do that. Our God is a God of second chances. He is a God of new beginnings. He is a God who believes so deeply in redemption that he sent his only Son to die on a cross for you. Pick yourself up. Change paths. Now. Let your first step be a short prayer asking for a second, third, and fifty-seventh chance. A sincere prayer asking for a new beginning. Let your second step be to keep reading this book.

The word education comes from the Latin word *educare,* which means to *draw out.* This is the aim of fine educators and educational experiences, driven by the belief that there is something unique and wonderful within each of us that is worth drawing out and sharing with the world. This is of course an inside-out approach.

Modern education has shifted to an outside-in approach that focuses more on teaching students *what* to think rather than *how* to think. This approach of imposing ideas and skills upon a student, rather than using the great thinkers of every age and vibrant conversation to draw out the best in each student, is driven by all the wrong motives. It is important to note that this is extremely unsettling to many teachers, who see what is happening, but feel limited by the system.

Our first educators are our parents. Many parents take the outside-in approach with their children because they simply don't know any better. They pass on what their own parents and other leaders in their lives taught them.

God is the ultimate Father and he is fully committed to the inside-out approach. He created each of us on purpose and for a purpose. He waits patiently and lovingly for the unique individual to emerge and embrace his or her mission in life. And he waits for you and me. But not passively. Along the way, God speaks to us, leading us, guiding us, correcting and disciplining us, coaching and encouraging us. He speaks.

I heard someone say recently, "God speaks to the world." I'm not sure that's true. I think God speaks to people. Our God is a deeply personal God. I have said it before, but I am compelled to repeat myself: Transforming people one at a time is at the heart of God's plan for the world.

One at a time. From the inside-out. Patiently. That's how God seeks to change the world. Through you and me, and others like us, one at time. And he speaks to us personally, individually, to lead us to the destiny he envisioned for us from the beginning of time.

Living from the inside-out versus the outside-in is a fundamental dichotomy that shapes our lives. It highlights the contrast between living an authentic life guided by what is good, true, beautiful, and just, in a quest for character and virtue, and living a superficial life driven by a desire for external validation, material success, and social status.

Living from the outside-in leads to a profound disillusionment and emptiness. Living from the inside-out leads a person to be able to say and believe, because they know it deep in their soul, "I am enough."

When we live from the outside-in, we often feel that we are not enough. Even people who are tremendously successful from a worldly perspective, if they are living from the outside-in, often experience a profound dissatisfaction with their lives and a persistent existential angst.

This enoughness, or lack thereof, is a simple indicator of where we stand in relationship with God. The love of God is not performative. We don't have to do anything to receive his love. He loves us no matter what. So, anytime we think we are less than enough, this is a clear indication that we are listening to voices other than his. The ultimate Father, the creator of all things including you, would never lead a son or daughter of his to believe that he or she is not enough.

The choice between living a life from the outside-in or from the inside-out is an easy one in theory once it has been properly explained. Yet, it is important to acknowledge and mourn the fact that most people in our society are now disadvantaged by not having had this fundamental dichotomy that shapes our lives explained to them.

But the choice is not a theoretical one. It is a choice we make many times each day, and often these choices are difficult and come at great personal cost. Just know at every turn that it is a price worth paying for—an integrated life, freedom, authenticity, inner peace, a strong sense of self, a life of substance, clear direction, and a profound sense of purpose and fulfillment.

Take a few minutes each day to listen to the three ordinary voices of God. He longs to lead you to live a beautiful life from the inside-out. Now let's explore how the second voice can help you do just that.

THE SECOND VOICE: THE BASICS

Talent is the second ordinary voice of God.

There are many people who think they have no talents. It's easy to see how they fall into this mistaken belief. We will speak shortly about why they feel that way. But it isn't true.

Each human being is endowed with a specific and particular set of gifts, talents, and abilities. They are divinely bestowed and intimately linked to a person's life mission.

When we are children, people ask us, "What do you want to be when you grow up?" As we get a little older, they ask, "What do you want to study in college?" And as graduation draws near, they ask, "What do you want to do when you graduate?" The people asking these questions are well meaning, but they are asking the wrong questions.

Want. Want. Want. Each question contains that word. Ask this dozens of times throughout a young person's life, and it conditions them to believe that life is about doing what you want to do. It isn't. Nobody ever found a life of fulfillment and happiness by doing what they wanted to do.

Life isn't about what we want to do. Each of these three questions exclude the possibility of vocation, calling, mission. And it is in these things that we find the unimaginable fulfillment for which every heart yearns but that so few ever experience.

What would be the right questions? They are so close and yet so far away from the common questions. What do you think God is calling you to be when you grow up? What do you think God wants you to study in college? What is God inviting you to dedicate your life to after graduation?

What is the difference between the two sets of questions? The first set places the focus on self. The second set of questions places the focus on God and a firm belief that God has created us for a specific purpose and equipped us with the talents and abilities necessary to carry out his assigned mission.

If we all focused a little more on what God wants and a little less on what we want, the world would be an astonishingly different place.

All talents come from God. Our talents can be immense and powerful. This often leads us to forget the first voice: need. Our talents can be so alluring that we deceive ourselves into believing that they are self-generated. This self-deception has led many people in every age to forget that "It is in him that we live, and move, and have our being." (Acts 17:28)

These talents can often be used to further the light or the darkness in this world. And people are often seduced into using their God-given talents for selfish ends. We also see individuals with immense talents—whose mental health is often disrupted in early life—use their God-given talents to unleash evil in the world. This is the price we pay for the extraordinary grace of freewill which makes love possible. The closer evil gets to us personally, the easier it is to fall into the mistaken belief that it is too high a price.

Talent is the second ordinary voice of God. We are made in the image of God, and as such, the creativity of God lives in each of us. It yearns for expression. To accompany these gifts, talents, and abilities, it is also important to note that as we are made in the image of God, these God-given talents are accompanied by God's own capacity for goodness, love, kindness, and generosity.

Your talents are clues, just like your needs are clues. Clues about how to live your life. Clues about how to live life to the fullest, how to be happy, how to live the abundant life that Jesus describes in the Gospel. These clues lead us to our unique mission.

EVERYBODY IS A GENIUS

Albert Einstein wrote, "Everybody is a genius. But if you judge a fish by its ability to climb a tree, it will live its whole life believing that it is stupid." The question I have for you at this part of our journey together is, "What is your genius?"

You see, I believe that we are all capable of doing one thing better than any other person alive at this time in history. What is your one thing?

I know what you may be thinking. You may be thinking quietly to yourself that you don't have a genius. You may be tempted to doubt the idea and think that I am talking only about the extraordinary people. No. Everybody is a genius. What's your genius?

Who are the extraordinary people, anyway? Are they the only ones who possess genius? Surely, we cannot count only those who achieve worldly acclaim and success.

If genius belongs only to those who invent things that change the whole course of human history, create masterpieces that draw crowds to art galleries for centuries, imagine symphonies that live on in our hearts forever, or become great presidents of great nations or great CEOs of great corporations—if we count only people who set world records and win gold medals, people who capture our imaginations and raise our spirits playing Major League Baseball or Basketball, those who win Oscars and Grammy Awards, and people who receive enormous public attention for going to heroic lengths to serve humanity— then what is to become of the rest of us? Are we to march off quietly, join Thoreau's masses, and lead lives of quiet desperation?

I think not.

Let me explain from another point of view. My mother lives in Australia, and probably nobody will ever write a book about my mother. She doesn't live in the right suburb on the right street, she doesn't drive an expensive car, and she didn't go to the right college. My mother never made a lot of money, she doesn't have a lot of money, she doesn't wear expensive clothes with fancy labels on them, she doesn't vacation in all the right places every year, and she hasn't had a job outside of the home since she gave birth to my oldest brother.

My mother hasn't invented anything that will change the whole course of human history, she is not the creator of artistic or musical masterpieces, and she has not, and is not likely to, become the great president of a great nation or corporation. Mum doesn't have any world records, gold medals, Oscars, or Grammy Awards, and she can go to the supermarket without being bothered by the paparazzi.

By all the world's standards, my mother is a failure. But let me assure you, my mother is a genius.

I remember as a child coming home from school. Every afternoon at 3:30 p.m. my seven brothers and I would descend upon the family home like some sort of invasion. Some of us had experienced triumph, and some of us had experienced tragedy. My mother was able to instantaneously console the tragedy and celebrate the triumph.

As one of eight children, I never felt like I was being treated as just part of the crowd. Both my mother and my father had a phenomenal ability to draw the best out of each of my brothers and me.

No. There will be no books about my mother. And as I said, if judged by all the world's standards, she is a complete failure. But you know what? My mother could not care less what the world thinks. Most people don't know her well enough to compliment her or criticize her. And she knows that. My mother could not care less what just about anybody thinks.

Do you know why? Because she knows who she is, and she knows why she is here. She has no illusions about trying to be someone she is not. My mother has discovered her genius, pursued her genius, exercised her genius, and celebrated her genius. And if you and I can get even the tiniest taste of the peace that comes from knowing that who we are, where we are, and what we are doing makes sense regardless of the outcome or other people's opinions—then we will have discovered our genius too.

Have we simply been judging ourselves by all the wrong criteria?

"Everybody is a genius. But if you judge a fish by its ability to climb a tree, it will live its whole life believing that it is stupid." What is your genius?

We are all capable of doing one thing better than any other person alive at this time in history. What is your one thing? Your one thing may be to love your spouse, raise your children, or be a kindergarten teacher.

Your one thing isn't your only thing. But it is the one thing.

Your one thing may be to invent something that changes the whole course of human history or to become the president of a great nation. It doesn't matter so much what form your genius takes as it does that you embrace and celebrate it.

How will you know when you discover your genius? There are two signs: joy and a feeling of timelessness. When I speak and when I write, the hours pass without notice. This is not work, it is passion. Is it always like that? No, of course not. There are times when to squeeze a single coherent paragraph from my mind takes hours and hours. But when I experience the joy and the timelessness of sharing these ideas, I know that I was born to share these ideas as a fish was created to swim or a bird to fly. It is simply a part of who I am. It is possible that you turned your back on your genius years ago. Many people cast aside their genius because it is not spectacular enough or because their family and friends wanted something different for them. All too often genius is abandoned because it doesn't make us enough money.

There is genius within you. We find it by listening to the voice of God in our lives. He speaks to us in many ways, and one of those ways is through our talents.

It isn't enough just to discover our talents. This is where many people get derailed in their journey. They discover their talents, but then abandon the giver of the gift. It is an astounding act of ingratitude to love the gift more than the giver of the gift. This is only magnified and multiplied when the giver of the gift is God.

It isn't enough just to discover our talents. The next step is to discern how God wishes us to express those talents in the world at this moment in history.

The three voices are linked in so many ways. We discover one here in our discussion of talents. The first voice is need. You have a legitimate need to discover and exercise your talents. You have a legitimate need to develop your talents. You have a legitimate need to find your genius and share it with the world.

God didn't give you your talents just for you. He entrusted them to you. But they are a gift he yearns to give to other people through you. It may be three people, or it may be three billion. One is not better than the other.

But if God's intention was for you to share your gift with three people, sharing it with three hundred could be extremely detrimental to you, the three people it was meant for, and the two-hundred and ninety-seven people you shared it with whom it wasn't intended.

It's a difficult paradox to get our minds around in this world where we measure everything and regularly fall into the trap of assuming that more is always better.

There will be times throughout this book when you will be tempted to think that it is too late for you to find your genius or that you have no genius. Let me make it unequivocally clear: Every evil force in this world and the next wants you to believe that. Those thoughts and feelings don't come from God, who with all the angels and saints, is showering you with the grace and wisdom necessary to do the next right thing.

One step in the right direction signifies a complete shift in momentum. It is time to shift the momentum of your life.

TWO TRUTHS

We all believe things about ourselves that aren't true. But if we stay open to the counsel of wise friends and listen to the voice of God in our lives, over time those who love us will unburden us of these things.

To explore the second ordinary voice of God it is necessary, even essential, to be very clear about two truths. And these two truths are often in direct opposition with two things many people believe about themselves that aren't true.

Many people believe they have no talents. It isn't true. The first truth is: You have abundant talents.

The reality is that God has given you so many talents that you cannot fully exercise even one of your talents in this lifetime. Fully exercise. Not even one. In your lifetime.

That's why it's essential that we turn to God from time to time and say, "Hey, God. What talent do you want me to focus on now? This year? For this stage or season of my life?"

Maybe you just became an empty nester—it's a good time to turn to God and say, "God, what talent do you want me to focus on at this time in my life?"

Maybe you just graduated from college—that's a good time to turn to God and say, "God, what talent do you want me to focus on at this time in my life?"

Maybe you've been stuck in a rut for a while. Perfect time to turn to God and say, "God, what talent do you want me to focus on at this time in my life?"

Well, you get the point. It is always a good time to turn to God and inquire about what he has planned for you next.

The second truth is: You've got all the talents you need.

But more than that, and here's the beautiful thing, you've got the perfect mix of talents that you need to fulfill the mission and live the life God created you for. There is no point worrying about the talents you don't have. It is in fact an insult to God's providence. And there is no point comparing your talents to the talents of your parents or siblings, your friends, teachers, colleagues, or anyone else. That is an exercise in futility and frustration.

You have the perfect mix of talents you need. If you don't have a talent, you don't need it.

If you needed a talent to live the incredible life he created you to live, God would have given it to you. Period. To suggest otherwise would be to question his astounding providence. God gave you the talents you need, and he speaks to you through those talents each day.

Now let's discover just how talented you are. I think most will be surprised at the breadth and depths of their gifts, talents, and abilities. And from this a new challenge will emerge: discerning which talents you should pursue in this season of your life and which to leave dormant for another season.

CONTEXT IS A BEAUTIFUL THING

I love context. If you ask a bunch of smart people for ideas to improve something you will get a lot of good ideas. In fact, almost every idea will seem like a good idea if you consider it in isolation. It's only when you put them side by side that you realize which are the truly great ideas and which are the duds. Putting those ideas side by side, that's context, and it's a beautiful thing.

Context shows us the true value of things. It delivers piercing clarity, clarity that can stop you in your tracks, clarity that will take your breath away. And that's why you should make context your very good friend.

Imagine for a moment you are the best football player in the world. You live and breathe football twenty-four hours a day. You work on the game, on your body, on strategy and plays for fifteen hours a day for most of the year. And yes, when you sleep, you dream about football. Wherever you go, you are known as the best of your generation. You're at the top of your game.

But then something happens. Your five-year-old son gets cancer. How important is football now? It's not important at all. You'd quit football, agree never to play football again, if it would cure your son. That's context.

Context shows us what matters most. Context shows us the true value of things.

God is constantly trying to put things in context for us. We go to church on Sunday, listen to the Gospel, and hear God saying, "I've been telling you for weeks now, that's not the most important thing, this is the most important thing."

The Gospel is constantly trying to rearrange our priorities by putting things in context, by showing us what matters most and what matters least. The Gospel teaches us the true value of things.

Wise men and women rearrange their priorities and organize their lives around the clarity that context provides.

What really matters? It's a huge question, but not an impossible question, especially with friends like context in our corner. Most people spend most of their lives confused about what really matters, and it doesn't have to be that way.

But clarity does require that we slow down a little. No, more than that. It requires that we pause to reflect on what is happening within us and around us, that we pause to put things in context before proceeding. Those pauses are prayer, reflection, meditation, long walks in quiet places, going to Mass, reading, and all the other ways we pause from the hustle and bustle of life to enter into holy leisure. This holy leisure radically increases our chances of living our lives well.

Who's the best in the world at creating context? The Catholic Church. It has a two-thousand-year record of creating context. It points out what matters most and challenges people and society to rearrange their priorities with unerring consistency. And it does it despite the fact that the person who provides the clarity of context is usually very, very unpopular.

But day in, day out, in every age, the Church stands up and announces what is true, good, beautiful, noble, just, and right. And she does it despite the massive wave of unpopularity that comes crushing down on her each time.

The Catholic Church is the best in the world at putting things side by side, the best in the world at pointing out the true value of things, the best in the world at putting things in context.

Who is the worst in the world at creating context? The media. To push their agendas and bolster their opinions, they willfully and negligently avoid putting things in context. You almost never see untampered with realities put side by side in the media. Why? Because the media doesn't want to give you context.

The more you understand the true value of things, the less likely you will be to waste your time consuming modern media. The media is not interested in the true value of things. They sold their souls for ratings, then advertising dollars, and now clicks.

The media used to be about presenting the news, a balanced view, and letting people think on it and decide for themselves. Do you remember what we said about shabby education when we were talking about living life from the inside-out or the outside-in? *Modern education has shifted to an outside-in approach that focuses more on teaching students what to think rather than how to think. This approach of imposing ideas upon a student, rather than using the great thinkers of every age and vibrant conversation to draw out the best in each student, is driven by all the wrong motives.*

Do you see a pattern emerging? Education, the media, and so many other aspects of our society have a vested interest in people living their lives from the outside-in. The powers that be not-so-secretly want people to be afraid, because fearful people keep coming back for more. And the more insecure we are, the more anxious and depressed we become, the more we base our value on external validation, the more inadequate we feel—the more we consume.

Context is a thing of beauty that should be sought and cherished once found. It shows us what matters the most, the true value of things, and that clarity is essential to our journey.

UNIQUE AND UNIVERSAL TALENT

Our gifts, talents, and abilities can be broken down into two groups: Universal talents and Unique talents.

Universal talents are talents that either everybody has, or the vast majority of people have.

An example would be the ability to make a difference in other people's lives. It's an incredible talent. If we pause to reflect on it, our ability to make a difference in other people's lives is an astounding talent.

But we discount it. We devalue it. Not consciously, necessarily, but unconsciously we devalue it.

Why? Well, because we're a little bit sick in the head. The truth is, we're all a little bit sick and sometimes we think sick little things in our sick little minds. We value the wrong things, we mis-value things, and we spend disproportionate amounts of time and energy on things that don't matter, while simultaneously neglecting things of astounding importance. As a result, we devalue universal talents just because they are universal.

And this is a perfect example. We know that God is the source of all talents. He gave us the extraordinary ability to make a difference in other people's lives, but we are dissatisfied with this gift and neglect it.

Because in our sick little minds we are thinking, *"Make a difference in other people's lives. God gave everyone that talent. If God really loved me, he would have given me some incredible talent, not this generic, one-size-fits-all 'Make a difference in other people's lives.' In fact, if God really, really loved me, he would have given me some astounding talent, and not only that, but he then would specifically and intentionally not give that talent to anybody else, ever again, in the history of the world."*

We devalue our universal talents because we think the fact that everyone has them makes them less important.

Here's another example. What do you love about your body? If you ask most people this question, they will first think about what they don't like about their body, and then to answer the question they will say my eye color, my height, my curves, my face, my smile, etc. But what are any of these compared to the ability to see? Or the ability to feel?

We favor the comparatively superficial over the substantial. The color of our eyes is irrelevant compared to our ability to see. We have a bias toward the particular and devalue the universal.

Now, let's consider the second type of talent: Unique talent.

This is where we tend to focus most of our attention as individuals and as a society. This single point has an outsized ability to distort our values, and it has.

What is unique talent? When the culture thinks of unique talent, they only consider the ability to write a symphony like Mozart or Beethoven; the ability to paint a picture like Van Gogh, Monet, or Picasso; the ability to cure a disease or invent something that changes the whole course of human history; or the ability to play football, baseball, or basketball better than 99.9% of people on the planet.

We all have unique talents. A talent doesn't have to make you rich and famous to be unique and powerful.

Everyone is good at something. We all have talents and abilities that are unique and different. These gifts are the key to great happiness in our lives and are sometimes leading indicators in our search to discover our vocation or mission in life. But first we must seek out these gifts and talents. So often people say to me, "But I am not good at anything." This I cannot believe. I can believe, however, that a person has not yet found that one area in which he or she has a special gift.

Our culture is obsessed with unique talents that make people rich and famous. But if you put these things side-by-side with the ability to make a difference they become trivial. Put being a great basketball player side by side with making a difference in other people's lives and it becomes clear that one is serious, and one is still, after all, a game.

In the grand scheme of things, making a difference in other people's lives is more important than being a great basketball player. But our culture is massively confused about this truth.

I find the proof of this truth in successful people. The overwhelming majority of people who become insanely successful at anything, and incredibly famous and wealthy in the process, then turn about and do what? Try to make a difference in other people's lives, and not just a few, but on an industrial scale, as many as possible.

They start a foundation, join a foundation, champion a cause, search for a cure, become an advocate or an activist, enter public service, champion education or the arts, or dedicate themselves to humanitarian aid and disaster relief.

They boldly, with fierce determination, set out to make a difference in the world with the same energy they set out to conquer their chosen field of success. Why? They could do what so many people fantasize about. They could sit around and do nothing all day. They could do whatever they wanted to do whenever they wanted to do it.

Why do people who are tremendously successful, who have become mind-blowingly famous and wealthy, people who could do whatever they wanted or nothing at all, why, almost universally, do they try to make a difference in other people's lives? Meaning. You cannot live a meaningful life by filling it with meaningless activities and things.

Why do they focus on making a difference in other people's lives? Because their lives are empty without that.

Our true humanity is realized through acts of kindness, empathy, compassion, generosity and service to others. Only by exploring our profound interconnectedness are we able to fully experience what it means to be human. Nigerian author and Nobel laureate, Wole Soyinka, observed, "You cannot become fully human until you start living for others."

Our need for meaning is colossal. We were made for meaning. We can't live happily without it. That's why we're drowning or suffocating, or both, in this shallow, superficial culture. We need meaning, we need a little bit of depth and seriousness. Both are profoundly agreeable to the human mind, body, heart, and soul.

Putting things side by side, that provides context—and context reveals the true value of things.

All this to prepare you for this one point: Your universal gifts, talents, and abilities may be infinitely more valuable than your unique gifts, talents, and abilities. Keep that in mind in your quest to listen to the second ordinary voice of God.

You are uniquely suited and superbly equipped to carry out your God-given mission. If you don't yet know what that mission is, use this time to prepare for the moment you discover it. Once you know what your mission is and what your talents are, never stop developing them.

Your life will have many different seasons. God has equipped you for all of them. Remember, God has given you so many talents that you cannot fully exercise even one of your talents in this lifetime. That makes it critically important that you turn to him from time to time and ask: God, which talent do you want me to focus on in this season of my life?

CHAPTER FOUR:
THE THIRD VOICE: DESIRES

THE POWER OF DESIRE

Desire is powerful. It is one of the more powerful forces at work within the human person. It can be harnessed for good or left to run amok.

Our desires play a powerful part in shaping our lives. Desire the wrong things and that alone will ruin your life. The power of desire attached to the wrong thing is like a runaway train—and that runaway train can be your life.

Most people rise or fall based their desires. Every scandal is a scandal of desire. It may not be physical desire, but the DNA of any scandal is desire run amok.

The wrong desire can destroy your life. So, choose your desires wisely.

There is a false ideology which asserts that we don't choose our desires, but rather that they emerge in us, and we have no choice. If this were true, it would be a horrendous and inhumane form of slavery. Yes, there are desires that emerge within us unbidden, but once they emerge, we get to choose what comes next.

Many of the egregious social problems that plague our society are the result of this false ideology.

What I need you to understand as we embark on this topic is that your power to desire is unfathomable. You get to choose how you direct that power.

Desire is best when focused. If you spread your desire among many things, it loses its strength, and is wasted.

The liberty you have when it comes to desire is that you get to choose where to focus it.

What is your desire focused on? What do you want it to be focused on? A new car, a better job, a watch, a handbag, pleasure, avoiding pain, a bigger house, the boy, the girl, true love, comfort, status, laziness, winning, more money, pleasing others, justice, success, the next big achievement, relieving suffering, the will of God..?

You get to decide. We choose the desires we focus on.

We spoke at the beginning of this book about the horrifying reality that it is possible, and disturbingly easy, to mis-live your life. One of the easiest ways to mis-live your life is to focus your immense power of desire on the wrong things.

What is God calling you to focus your unfathomable power of desire on at this time in your life? Allow God to speak to you through your desires. Ask yourself: Is this desire from God? Learn to discern the difference between desires God has placed in your heart and desires that the culture has placed in your heart.

People say, "God is good." It is true. But God is also more than good, he is Goodness. The wise man or woman desires God above all else. At this moment, it might be impossible for you to grasp that concept, and that's okay. Just know that the wise man, and the wise woman, began walking the path of wisdom by desiring good.

Give the desire for good a firm place in your mind, heart, and soul. Desire good for yourself and your family, desire good for your community and country, desire good for your friends and for strangers.

The power of desire is unfathomable. It will surprise you at times and leave you stunned and amazed at other times. Use that power within you for good.

THE THIRD VOICE: THE BASICS

Desire is the third ordinary voice of God. But not just any desire—

deepest desire. God has placed desires for good deep in your heart, and he speaks to you through those deep desires for good things.

The problem is the world fills our hearts with a plethora of shallow and superficial desires.

The first challenge is to dig through all the shallow and superficial desires so we can discover the deep desires. The second is to live our lives from that deepest part of the self where our truest desires reside.

A simple example. Around lunchtime each day, I've got desires. I desire a burger, some fries, and an RC Cola (that's a long story for another day). These are shallow desires for pleasure and comfort. I have a deeper desire for health and well-being. If I act out of my deeper desires, I choose something healthier from the menu.

Each time we choose to live out our deeper desires, we expand our capacity for everything that is good, true, right, just, and noble. When we side with our shallow and superficial desires, our capacity for these things contracts.

This dynamic plays out dozens of times a day in our lives. Too often we side with our shallow desires, having disastrous effects on our individual lives and on society as a whole—but most of all this dynamic has a disastrous impact on our souls.

People who don't know what they want are dangerous. People who want everything are dangerous. People who want the wrong things are dangerous. And people who want the right things for the wrong reasons are dangerous.

The world needs people who want the right things for the right reasons.

The ability to focus our desire on anything we choose is an astounding ability. It's one of those universal talents we spoke about in the previous chapter. Once you become aware of these universal talents, you discover there are a lot more of them than you realized upon first examination.

It's time to start digging through the many shallow and superficial desires the world has burdened our hearts with. It's time to discover the deepest desires God has placed in our hearts. It is time to acknowledge that he placed them in our hearts for a reason, and that he continues to speak to us through those deep desires for good. And it is time to unleash the power of desire by aligning our thoughts, words, actions, and choices with the deepest desires of our hearts.

People often ask, "What do you think I should do with my life?" We almost always ask the wrong person. It is a question best directed toward God in prayer.

God uses the three ordinary voices to speak to us every single day of our lives. There are no exceptions. There are no days when he doesn't speak to you in these ways, and there is no one he doesn't speak to.

One of the most beautiful aspects of this discussion is that our needs, talents, and desires are vocational. They point out the path God created us to walk.

What should I do with my life? Your whole life may be before you and you may be asking this question seriously for the first time. Or you may be much farther along the path and asking, "What should I do with the rest of my life?" Whatever the case may be, listen to God speaking to you through your needs, talents, and desires, and the direction you are seeking will emerge.

THE TRIVIAL MANY VS. THE ESSENTIAL FEW

Less is more. You've heard it before. But did you also know that less is better? We live in a culture of more, more, more, so most people have never paused to consider the virtues of less. When it comes to your God-given ability to desire, less is both more and better.

Life isn't about getting more done in less time, it's about focusing on those very few things that God intended for you. These are the vital few.

Cast aside the trivial many and embrace the vital few. This is an essential step in any serious spiritual journey.

What is essential? This is the question a finite being living a finite life is forced to consider in a world of unlimited opportunities and possibilities.

What is essentialism? It is the approach a reasonable person takes upon discovering that he or she is a finite being living a finite life in a world of unlimited opportunities and possibilities.

Essentialism is about giving priority to what matters most and letting go of what matters least. It's about asking the question: What is essential for your health, happiness, and wholeness? And it's about choosing the people and things that are essential for your health, happiness, and wholeness over the many trivial and superficial time and energy vampires that suck all the passion and purpose out of your life.

Maybe a little less in almost every area of your life is the secret to the rare fulfillment that we all yearn for but so few of us find. But maybe a lot less is what is called for. The question is: Will you live your life in the service of the trivial many or the vital few?

The vital few are what God created you to experience.

Perhaps you are already an essentialist. It's possible. But if you are constantly feeling overwhelmed, if you are always trying to do more with less, if you believe that if you procrastinated less and were more efficient you would be able to get everything done—you are not an essentialist. Though it does sound like you could benefit considerably from becoming one.

Still not sure? Okay. Let's take a closer look. Let's explore the difference between an essentialist and a non-essentialist.

The non-essentialist rushes around trying to be all things to all people. The essentialist tries to be a great friend to a few people.

The non-essentialist engages in the undisciplined pursuit of more. The essentialist engages in the disciplined pursuit of less. The non-essentialist is never satisfied. The essentialist has taken time to explore what will deliver contentment.

The non-essentialist thinks, "I have to." The essentialist thinks, "I choose to."

The non-essentialist thinks, "It's all important." The essentialist thinks, "Only a few things really matter."

The non-essentialist is constantly reacting to what's urgent. The essentialist focuses on what's truly important, and the most important things in life are almost never urgent.

The non-essentialist says yes without really thinking about it. The essentialist says no to everything except what is essential.

The non-essentialist takes on too much and does nothing well. The essentialist does less and delivers excellence.

The non-essentialist's life feels out of control. The essentialist's life feels measured and manageable.

The non-essentialist constantly feels overwhelmed and exhausted. The essentialist has learned to enjoy the journey.

The non-essentialist is tossed about by his or her trivial desires. The essentialist can set aside their many trivial desires in order to cherish their deepest desires.

Are you ready to give priority to what is essential? Are you ready to start saying no to all the stuff that in the long run won't mean anything to anyone? Does the idea appeal to you? Does just hearing about it stir your soul? Then maybe, just maybe, it's time you became an essentialist.

FROM FOMO TO JOMO

Your desires are many, but your *deepest* desires are very few. When it comes to desire, God invites us to focus on the vital few and cast aside the trivial many. But he promises that the vital few will be more satisfying than the trivial many.

The key to achieving this transition is letting go of FOMO and embracing JOMO.

This is a topic I have written about before, but I feel compelled to revisit it here because it is critical to understanding the joy that comes from listening to God's voice.

Without the purposeful determination of an essentialist, we are destined to live a life of distraction. One hundred and fifty years ago, Henry David Thoreau left Concord, Massachusetts because he believed it had become too noisy, too busy, too distracting. He went out to Walden Pond to reconnect with himself and with nature. It took him only seven pages in his writings to conclude that, "Most men lead lives of quiet desperation."

Today, most men and women lead lives of distraction. Lack of focus leads to lack of commitment, and together these lead us to lives of quiet (and not so quiet) desperation.

Essentialism challenges us to name what matters most. It gives us the clarity and wisdom to focus on the vital few rather than chasing the trivial many. And it liberates us from all the distraction and superficiality that dominates the culture.

I had a college roommate who was constantly running from one thing to the next, sacrificing sleep, and neglecting schoolwork. One day I asked him why he was choosing this path, and he said to me, "I don't want to miss out on anything during these four years." This state has come to be known as FOMO—Fear of Missing Out.

The idea that if we make the right choices, squeeze enough into each day, and become ultra-efficient, we won't miss out on things is a colossal error. More than an error, it is a delusion. You are going to miss out. In fact, you are certain to miss out on the great majority of things, experiences, and opportunities.

One of the biggest traps you can fall into is FOMO. Driven by the psychological nonsense of FOMO, many people make the worst decisions of their lives.

FOMO also has a close cousin known as "settling." The accepted wisdom of the vast universe known as the Internet is that you should never settle. This is horrible advice. The two most common expressions of this nonsense relate to relationships and career. "Settling" romantically means committing to someone who is less than ideal for you. The professional version of this nonsense involves "settling" for a job that pays the bills and supports your family rather than pursuing your dreams.

The truth is this: You have to settle. You don't have a choice. It is unavoidable. Our lives are finite. You do not have infinite time on this earth to pursue all possibilities. Your time is limited. You cannot become successful at anything without first settling on that path. To become a successful teacher or doctor, you set aside the possibilities of other careers and commit yourself to being a teacher or a doctor. If you bounce from one career to the next, never mastering any particular craft, you are "settling" in a different, much more diabolical way.

One of the main reasons so many young people are increasingly having trouble maintaining significant romantic relationships is because they want to keep all their options open. But keeping all your options open shuts down the possibility of success in the one relationship you are in at this moment.

Many people never arrive at the vital few because they refuse to settle, and as we have seen, settling is unavoidable. Every decision is a decision to miss out. Every choice for something is a choice to miss out on everything else.

FOMO and "settling" both foster unrealistic ideals that nobody can live up to due to the innate limitations of life and all human beings. The result is a growing anxiety because we are constantly missing out and settling is inevitable.

It is preferable to miss out on most things, because the only things that really matter are those that God has in mind just for you. Doing the will of God, therefore, transforms FOMO into JOMO—the Joy of Missing Out.

This wisdom is essential if we are going to learn to hear the third ordinary voice of God: Desire.

DESIRE AND THE FOUR ASPECTS

Desire has been one of the most misunderstood facets of the human person in the context of spirituality throughout history. But just as to be human is to need, to be human is to desire. This is often overlooked. In fact, it is often forgotten that our God who created us marvelously and wonderfully, created us with desires. The higher truth, the more interesting path to pursue here, is that our desires have the propensity to connect this world and the next.

A brief journey through the four aspects of the human person reveals that desire figures significantly in each aspect. From the practical to the profound, our human desires at times reach for the dirt, but yearn to reach for the divine.

But before we dive headlong into the ocean of human desire, it is crucial to recognize that the wisest men and women of every age and every tradition have learned to desire their legitimate needs before everything else. Some came quickly to the realization, others came kicking and screaming, but one and all, sooner or later, came to two profound understandings:

1. Unless a cross-section of our legitimate needs is satisfied—physically, emotionally, intellectually, and spiritually—we are unable

to flourish regardless of how many of our other desires get fulfilled; and,

2. The satisfaction of a need may not be spectacular, but it is almost always more fulfilling in the long run to have the simplest needs satisfied on a regular basis than it is to achieve a once-in-a-lifetime accomplishment that you have desired for your whole life. Both have their place, but the regular satisfaction of our simplest needs often outshines the satisfaction of a single grand desire.

This is to say, even as we continue to delve into the many spheres of human desire, let us not forget that desiring what we need before desiring what we want is a mark of wisdom.

Physical Desire

Raise the word "desire" in our culture and the assumption is that you are speaking of sexual desire. This is an important aspect of human desire, but to view all desire through this lens is a mistake. In fact, to even use sexual desire as a starting point is a mistake. But our hyper-sexualized culture would like the conversation about human desire to start and end there.

Many of your physical desires fall into the category of luxury needs. For example, the homes and apartments that the great majority of us live in far outstrip our basic need for shelter and fall firmly in the camp of a desire fulfilled. Comfort is the physical desire that leads us to make homes for ourselves that go far beyond what we actually need. It is important to note, this is not a criticism of this. It is however necessary to keep a clear delineation between what is a need and what is a want.

Our quest to explore physical desire at every turn is going to be burdened with our desire for pleasure. The great majority of our physical desires are for some form of pleasure, comfort, or sexual gratification.

I enjoy these things as much as the next person. And I believe God wants us to enjoy these things within the appropriate context. But our culture has promoted pleasure as the ultimate end in life and that is an error. Pleasure is not the supreme good that this life has to offer us.

This is quickly discovered by asking: Does pleasure bring us meaning and purpose? It does not and therefore is not the ultimate aim of life. Overindulgence in pleasure, comfort, or sexual gratification does not produce a man of whom we can say, "He has mastered the art of being a human being," or a woman of whom we could say, "She provides a role model for all young women on the best way to live life."

We need to be constantly looking for the desire beyond the desire. Earlier in this chapter, we discussed my lunchtime desire for burgers and fries. But beyond this shallow desire for pleasure and comfort, we discovered I had a deeper desire for health and well-being. This is the desire beyond the desire.

The only way to say no to anything is to have a deeper yes. And you will need to deny a great many of your desires unless you wish for your life and soul to run amok. The desire beyond the desire provides the next clue, over and again, until finally we arrive at the ultimate desire (of which we will speak shortly).

There is a hierarchy of desire. Some desires are higher than others, and some are lower than all. Our physical desires, as we will soon see, rank low in this hierarchy. This is merely an observation, not a criticism. The human race would not be perpetuated without these desires, so let's not pretend they don't have a place, and a vitally important place at that.

Emotional Desires

The instant gratification that can often be developed in the realm of physical desire will make it quite impossible to explore and master the realm of emotional desire. The reason is this: The finest fruits of the emotional world are reserved for those willing to participate patiently and selflessly.

What is an example of one of these emotional desires?

We desire friendship. This desire is driven by many motives, but among them is a desire to have a small group of companions to share our joys and sorrows with. When good things happen to us, our natural instinct is to share our good fortune with others. This is one of the reasons the Gospels of Jesus Christ are often referred to as the Good News, because anyone who has an authentic encounter with Jesus finds it impossible not to share this good news with anyone who crosses his or her path.

Sharing our joy magnifies the joy.

On the other hand, when we encounter the underbelly of humanity and life, we yearn to share our pain and suffering. When we are touched by hardship, violence, betrayal, illness, natural disaster, loneliness, addiction—we don't want someone to tell us what we should have done differently, or the mistakes we have made, or recount the times we ignored their advice. What we desire is to be able to sit down with a friend, or perhaps a small group of companions, to share with them the way that evil has touched or encroached upon our life this day. All we seek in return is for that person or people to say, "We see you. We hear you. We are with you. We care. You are worthy."

Sharing our heartache diminishes our pain, suffering, and anguish.

What is the desire? To share the feelings caused by a person or situation. Suppressed as this desire may be in some people, we have a firm desire to share our feelings with others.

Your desire to express your feelings is only the tip of the iceberg of your larger desire to be heard, loved, accepted, and understood. Learning to express your feelings to the right person, at the right time, in the right setting is a prerequisite for the fulfillment of your many emotional desires.

This of course is just the beginning of the labyrinth which represents our emotional desires. They are many. We desire intimacy, autonomy, trust, joy, security, stability, conversation, love, acceptance, affection, respect, admiration, attention, compassion, encouragement, honesty, empathy, and connection.

Our emotional desires are many, and they change from one season of our lives to another. The essential thing to keep in mind is that your desires are a unique part of your journey. They are emerging in you at this time for a specific reason. Would you like to know what that specific reason is? Only by listening to your desires and discussing them with God will you be able to comprehend the place they have in your onward journey.

Intellectual Desires

Do you love learning?

Somewhere along the way, most people have been told that they are stupid or not smart enough, or that their education is insufficient, or they've been intellectually flogged by someone with all the right degrees from all the right places, who is sickeningly arrogant and elitist, and yet, staggeringly insecure. But most people are robbed of their love of learning by the systems and structures that focus on memorization, testing, and being told what to think instead of being taught how to think.

All this discourages a love of lifelong learning, which is one of the sources of unmitigated joy in this life.

The first step is to set aside all the pseudointellectual bullying you have ever experienced. It would be great if we could just press a button that says, "Restore Factory Settings." It would be a great name for a book actually. It would be a fun book to write the more I think about it. But the point is, you were created with a set of dispositions and abilities that you have neglected, given away, or had stolen along the way and it's time to get them back.

The first is your intellectual capacity. It is significant. Greater than most people realize. And yet, most people put it away too early in life. Nobody has reached the limits of their intellectual capacity. Most people just quit developing it.

"You think too much," may be one of the worst phrases in the history of the world. And it is certainly on the top-ten list of the worst things to say to a teenager or adolescent who is hastily trying to figure out who she is, and what life is, and her role in all of that.

Thinking is good. More is better. There can of course be too much, but do you have any idea how few people are in any danger of crossing that line? Not 1%. Not 1% of 1%. Less.

The problems we face both as individuals and collectively as a society will not be solved with shallow, superficial thinking. They won't be solved by consuming soundbites and putting together a philosophy of life based on a conglomerate of all those soundbites.

The problems we face require deep thought. Not the deep thought of one person, or even a great group of people. They will be solved only if we raise the quality and depth of thought of most people in our society.

It is necessary to say all this before we address your intellectual desires. Many people struggle to name their intellectual desires. One reason for this is that in order for a culture to assert the dominance of sexual desires it first has to decimate people intellectually. Any culture that wants to control or excessively influence people's behavior must first suppress the critical thinking function. But still, just below the surface, ready to grow again at any time, are your intellectual desires.

Intellectual desire is best understood in the example of a child.

Children have a curiosity that brings a natural sense of wonder to their lives. They are eager to understand, and they yearn for knowledge.

From the moment children can think and speak logically, one question dominates their inner dialogue (thoughts) and their outer dialogue (conversations). Internally and externally, they are constantly asking, *Why?* They are naturally curious, eager to understand, and they yearn for knowledge.

Intellectual desire is one of the great signs of human flourishing. If you have lost it, it is time to get it back.

It is also necessary to point out that while people have access to more content than ever, they are reading more fear-inducing, soul-destroying content than ever.

The content we consume has radically changed in one generation. We now have people who claim to be committed readers who haven't cracked the cover of a book in five years. Online short form articles based on opinions and agendas do not provide the stimulation and sustenance necessary to fulfill your intellectual desires. There are many reasons for this, but the screen itself and its ability to distract you is reason enough.

There is something about sitting down alone in a quiet place with a good book.

One sentence. Let's dissect it.

"There is something about"—It's impossible to say what that something is. Is it mysterious and mystical? Yes. Both. Is it also eminently practical? Absolutely. And perhaps the something represents the potential of all that is yet unseen, unheard, and undiscovered in you.

"Sitting down"—To sit is to be at leisure. Leisure is essential for deep thought. It is a quality lost in a modern, utilitarian culture that has no respect for the fruits born from regular encounters with leisure, for such fruits take too long to grow and they awaken us and warn us that the direction society has taken is a dangerous one.

"Alone"—Jesus repeatedly sought places where he could be alone. It happened so often and with such regularity throughout each of the four Gospels that to ignore the practice in our own lives brings into question our status as disciples and students of the Great Master.

"In a quiet place"—If we wish to make the journey from chaos to order, and the journey from confusion and clarity, silence will be an indispensable ingredient. I often imagine God calling to me, "Come to the quiet."

"With a good book"—If you feed your mind garbage, you can expect your life to become no better. Improve the quality of the content you feed your mind each year, and you will be amazed at the outsized impact this one shift will have on your life. Not every book is a good book, and there are too many to read them all. The secret is to find the books that will meet you where you are and lead you to where God is calling you.

Every year, Dynamic Catholic publishes an overall TOP TEN list of books, but also separate lists specifically for men, women, and children. Visit www.DynamicCatholic.com to explore the lists.

If you are not in tune with your intellectual desire, what happened? Maybe as a child your parents used to yell at you when you asked questions. Perhaps you always wanted to learn to play the piano, but your friends told you it was only for sissies. The simplest things can cause us to shrink back and bury ourselves. You asked a question in class as a child, all the other children laughed, and the embarrassment buried your natural intellectual desire to learn continuously.

Life doesn't spare any of us from these and other bitter—sometimes brutal—experiences. Still, we have to get back up and move on. In this case, that means rediscovering our intellectual desires. Leisure brings clarity to the mind. Allow yourself time to rest, relax, and be rejuvenated. As you do, your intellectual desires will once again begin to emerge. It doesn't need to be days or weeks. It could be two hours on Sunday afternoon at the same time each week.

Our intellectual desire is great. And before we close, I feel compelled to warn you about one pitfall. Many people I speak with explain to me that their intellectual desires and needs are met through their professional work. This assessment may seem reasonable at first glance, but the reality is this scenario poses a serious threat to your overall well-being.

Let me explain. There are very few people whose professional development is in alignment with authentic human development and the spiritual development our faith provides. If such professional development is not in alignment, it is out of alignment. To defend your integrity and dignity, it is critical that your spiritual-intellectual development be at least equal to your professional-intellectual development. Without this balance, the inevitable result will be that you and your life will be dragged further and further out of alignment with your values and priorities. A car with increasingly poor alignment will end up in a ditch sooner or later.

How fully alive do you feel intellectually at this time in your life? Increase your intellectual engagement by reading one good spiritual book each month for a year. That amounts to about five pages a day, and that will change your life.

Nurture your intellectual desires. Feed your mind.

The final expression of human desire to explore is spiritual desire. But to fully understand the dynamics of spiritual desire it is first necessary to explore a crucial question.

THE WANT BEYOND THE WANT

Behind every desire is a more revealing desire.

Most people don't have the foggiest idea what they want. That isn't a judgment, it's just an observation. It isn't their fault. Perhaps they were never taught how to want, and what to want, and why wanting some things is better than wanting others. But now we are here, and it turns out, knowing what you want matters. And it matters a lot.

If you ask people what they want, they will give you an answer that is vague, general, and unimpeachable (at least from a worldly perspective). "I want to win the lottery." Or they will give you an answer that tells you the next thing they want, the next rung on their ladder of desire, but does not actually reveal their true desire. "I'd like a promotion." Others will propose something so completely unattainable that it abdicates them of any responsibility to pursue it.

Others have thought long and hard about the question, and their answers reflect that. "I really want to be a good father." "I want a better marriage. I know it's important, but I've been deprioritizing it for so long I don't know where to start." "I know my body is a temple of the Holy Spirit and I'd like to learn how to treat it more respectfully."

Others still will answer in the negative. "I don't want to be broke anymore." "I don't want to feel trapped." "I don't want to feel anxious and depressed anymore." "I don't want to be alone."

In order to discover what you want in any meaningful way, the first thing you need to do is give yourself some runway. It takes 7,500 feet of runway to raise a Boeing 747 jet into the air, and you need about the equivalent of existential runway to figure out what it is you want.

There is a beautiful verse in the Book of Proverbs that I return to time and time again. "Where there is no vision, the people will perish." (Proverbs 29:18) If you feel like you are perishing, even in small ways, there is a better than even chance that you are without a vision.

It's time for some visioning.

The first step is to get clear about your primary values. There's no point having a list of 192 things. The purpose of these primary values is to use them as navigational instruments throughout your day. You need to be able to pause for a moment in the middle of a busy day and ask, "Does what I am considering doing align with my values?" Perhaps your primary values are patience, kindness, humility, generosity, and love. When deciding what to do in a given situation, you measure what you are thinking of doing against those values and see if they line up.

These values are necessary for visioning. Choose three, four, or five for yourself. I don't recommend more than five.

The next step is to get beyond the current nonsense that is dominating your life. Visioning isn't problem solving. They are two very different activities. One is focused on an immediate situation and the other focuses on your future. If you don't choose a timeframe beyond your current set of messy circumstances, you won't do any visioning. You will get wrapped up in problem solving.

Your better future is beyond your current nonsense and messy circumstances. That's why your visioning timeline needs to be far enough off in the distance that you don't need to think about these things, or far enough off that you are confident you can deal with your existing nonsense and circumstances.

Imagine your life one year from now. What do you want to be doing? Who do you want to be spending your time with? Where do you want to be? How are you a better human being one year from now if you abide by your self-selected values?

Write it all down. Don't judge what you want. You can sort the wheat from the chaff later. Don't just write down all the good stuff. The human heart is divided and yearns for things that can destroy it. There is no point pretending. That's just a waste of time. Be honest. Even about your selfish desires. Even about your dark desires. Ignoring them won't make them go away. Naming them will allow you to understand them, perhaps not completely, but partially, and gradually. And this is the only way to learn to direct them and integrate them in a healthy way. Write down the selfish things you want to do and have and experience. Bring them into the light. That's how we deal with them. The good, the bad, the ugly—just write it down.

Next, do the same thing for three years from now and five years from now.

I have led tens of thousands of people through this exercise. I have been helping people envision a bigger and better future for three decades. But one thing dawned on me recently: Your better future may be a smaller future.

This is radically counter intuitive to everything our culture teaches us, which is always "more" and "bigger." You may never have considered it before, so it might be time to consider the possibility that your better future might be a smaller future.

What do you want? It seems like a simple question. It isn't. It is an extraordinarily difficult question to answer.

The temptation is to settle for false certainty. Our minds sometimes prefer false certainty to the uncomfortable tension produced by uncertainty.

We often see this with high school students. Some will claim to know with absolute certainty what they are going to do with the rest of their lives even though they are only fourteen or sixteen years old. They might know. But they may just be so uncomfortable with uncertainty that they force themselves to decide, preferring the false certainty over the honest uncertainty of the situation.

What do you want? Why is this question so difficult to answer? Because it's like a piece of string that a puppy dog has gotten a hold of and is proceeding to unravel the whole roll of string.

The secret is uncovering the want beyond the want.

A friend of yours is looking for love. If you ask her what she is looking for, she will tell you confidently and clearly, that she wants to get married to a particular type of man, but that these three things are non-negotiables for her. . . and she lists them.

The search goes on for years. The unfulfilled search becomes the primary source of angst in her life and the place she goes to dump all her head trash.

But despite all this, the desired man does eventually enter her life. He meets all the criteria. He passes the non-negotiables test. He pays attention to her, he wants to help her dreams come true, and he cherishes her more than she ever imagined a man would.

Your friend who was looking for love has found love ... but ... something is still missing.

What was the want beyond the want? She may have been aware of it, but in many cases, people are oblivious to these desires that are buried deep in the unconscious.

What was the want beyond the want? Self-love. She didn't love herself. Your friend thought that if she found the right man, if she found love, something would change. She hoped that he would love her, and she would love him, and somewhere in all of that she would learn to love herself. But she didn't.

There are ways to learn to love ourselves as God loves us, but romantic relationships are rarely the place to do that.

Another friend wants to be successful. He is driven and hardworking. He obsesses over his road to success. He can never relax and enjoy the present moment, because the pull of the future is too great. He works harder than any person you have ever met for a decade, perhaps two. And finally, he makes it, he reaches the pinnacle he chose to claim. He owns the business he always wanted to own, or has the role he wanted to have, or perhaps he has the net worth he set out achieve...

But ... something is still missing.

"What's the matter with you?" you ask him. "You have everything you always wanted."

The problem is the undiscovered want beyond the want.

What was his want beyond the want? He had a father who told him he would never succeed at anything, and a mother who refused to be proud and impressed because it took attention away from her.

What was the want beyond the want? He wanted his parents to love him and be proud of him. But his father was dead, and his mother was too much of a narcissist and therefore incapable of satisfying your friend's very real needs and desires.

And so, we have come to the dead end that so many people come to. The dead end of getting what we want. They arrive here by asking over and again, what do I want? They make the effort and do the work. It is impressive and admirable because many others give up along the way. But these few make it to the dead end and become disillusioned because they thought it would be more fulfilling to get what they wanted.

It isn't really a dead end. But sadly, there are so few guides willing or able to take people beyond the dead end of getting what we want.

The secret is to keep asking a different question, forever, in every situation and in new and different ways: What is the want beyond the want?

Are you ready to discover the ultimate answer to that question?

CHAPTER FIVE:
THE ULTIMATE DESIRE

THAT NAGGING FEELING

When you were a child, you had dreams for your future. As you grew older those dreams changed. Somewhere along the way you stopped dreaming and started focusing on the realities of everyday life. We all do. You had bills to pay, went looking for work, had to find somewhere to live, and your dreams got crowded out.

And yet, every once in a while, there is a nagging feeling that interrupts you when you're cooking, shaving, driving to work, watching your children play soccer, or late at night when you can't sleep. And that nagging feeling is accompanied by the thoughts and questions: Is this it? I have more to offer. Something's missing. There must be more to life. What am I doing wrong?

Sound familiar?

You quietly curse that nagging feeling and try to think about something else. You think it is criticizing you. It isn't. You think it is telling you that you failed. You didn't fail. You think it is an enemy. It isn't. Quite the opposite. It is a good and true friend.

That nagging feeling is the great equalizer.

It will gnaw at you whether you are the CEO of a multi-national corporation or selling drugs on a street corner. It pays no heed to our wealth or poverty, to our sickness or health, to our age or nationality. It doesn't care if you just got dumped or married, just got a promotion or fired, just won the lottery or filed for bankruptcy, just scored the winning touchdown in the Superbowl or suffered a career-ending injury.

It will go on reminding you that you do have more to offer, that something is missing, that there is more to life, and that you were made for more.

And somewhere deep inside, you know that nagging feeling is right.

You might tell yourself that it would go away if only you had more money, different friends, more pleasure, more accomplishments, or more possessions. But it won't.

You want to fix it or make it go away. You want to give it what it wants, but nobody ever taught you how to do that.

You try to convince yourself that what you really need to do is upend your life and pursue your childhood dreams. But that's not it either. Our childhood dreams serve us by teaching us how to dream. But our young hearts rarely stumble upon the ultimate dream.

What if the unconsidered dream is the only one worth pursuing?

It may seem hard to believe, but one unexplored possibility is more crucial and delightful than all the rest. And it is that unconsidered dream that needs your consideration now.

That nagging feeling will continue to gnaw at you until you get it right. That's its job. It cares about you too much to stop.

Get what right? Good question. Your heart's dominant desire.

YOUR HEART'S DOMINANT DESIRE

Let me explain. We spoke earlier about the vital few and the trivial many. We discussed how important it is to abandon the trivial many and pursue the vital few. But this path doesn't end with the vital few.

We need to escape the trivial many first in order to realize that many of our desires are trivial. This teaches us that there is a hierarchy of desire. All desires are not equal, and if that is true, one desire must be superior to all others.

Culling our herd of desires helps bring into view the ultimate summit. Once we learn to discard our trivial desires, we are able to continue narrowing them down until we arrive at the summit of singular desire. The peak of the spiritual life.

Our quest is a path to the singular. We are in search of the one and only desire that will satisfy our restless, confused, and lonely hearts.

There is always one dominant desire in our hearts. It's often the wrong one, usually of secondary importance, but there is always one desire that dominates. Not two or three or five. One.

Our hearts were made for singular devotion. They don't do well when we try to focus them on many things. They thrive on singular focus.

W. Clement Stone observed, "Definiteness of purpose is the starting point of all achievement." Most people never get there. It is life's greatest tragedy, for to live our whole lives without this definiteness of purpose is to half-live at best and to mis-live at worst.

But the great majority of people never bring their lives into focus. They dabble in this and that, they dabble in all manner of things, but never focus their hearts on the singular desire beyond every desire. This isn't a judgment, just an observation. I don't blame them. They were never taught what we are discussing now.

It's time to stop dabbling. Are you ready?

You cannot live life to the fullest without establishing this singular desire. One desire above all others. One desire for which you are willing to sacrifice all others.

Pursuing your one white-hot desire can only be achieved with singular focus. Too many desires spread too thin leads to the phenomenon we call lukewarm.

This white-hot burning desire isn't for physical pleasure. The limitations of physical pleasure simply lead us to the higher reality of spiritual pleasure. The primary limitation of physical pleasure is that it cannot be sustained beyond the activity producing it, and that activity cannot be sustained continuously. And we desire continuous pleasure because we were created for continuous pleasure. Not physical pleasure, spiritual pleasure.

Your heart needs the clarity and intentionality of a singular dominant desire. This is the answer to that nagging feeling.

You have tried pursuing singular dominant desires in the past. You may have focused your heart on a love interest or an accomplishment, a specific material possession or a certain type of physical pleasure. But these never worked. They never do. They can't. They are incapable. And you were left wanting more because you were made for more.

We all want our lives to change. Perhaps not completely, but in some way. But we are sick patients who refuse to take the medication that will heal us.

Have you ever known someone who refused to take medication they desperately needed? If you have then you have the shadow of a glimpse of how frustrated God must be with us at times.

UNANSWERED QUESTIONS

And so, we are left with three unanswered questions.

How do we change our lives?

What is the want beyond every want?

What is the singular dominant desire we should focus our hearts on?

The first one is easy. We change our lives by changing the central object of our attention. The second and third questions share the same answer. Let's explore that answer and then we will return to discuss how we shift the central object of our attention.

Pope John Paul II was elected as the 264th successor of Saint Peter on October 16, 1978. In June of the following year, he returned to his beloved Poland to visit a suffering people. For nine days the new pope electrified the country and signaled to the whole world that his papacy would be like none other.

Catholicism had been a rich part of Poland's history. More than just a religion, many considered the Church to be the repository of Polish culture and the protector of Polish tradition during the country's long periods of foreign domination.

Poland was still under Communist Russian rule when Pope John Paul II visited in 1979. The Soviet government warned him not to come, but he would not be persuaded, and the political, spiritual, and historic impact of his visit reshaped modern Poland.

The official position of the Communist Party was that religion was "the opium of the masses" and that faith was both irrelevant and unnecessary. Teachers were instructed to tell their students that Pope John Paul II was a dangerous enemy and Polish media coverage was heavily censored to limit the pope's exposure in his homeland.

But his message was crisp, clear, and compelling, and over those nine historic days when the people of Poland came out in record numbers to welcome him home and to celebrate their persecuted faith and country together. 300,000 people attended his opening Mass in Victory Square. More than three million attended his final Mass eight days later in Krakow.

Pope John Paul II asked the crowds if they were willing to take on the responsibilities of the faith amid their country's current circumstances. And what did these huge crowds who lived under the scrutiny and threats of communism reply? They spontaneously thundered back, "We want God! We want God!"

There is the answer to our questions.

What is the want beyond every want? God. What is the singular dominant desire we should focus our hearts on? God.

THIS IS HOW WE CHANGE OUR LIVES

So, how do we reorient our lives singularly toward God? How do we change the central object of our attention?

This is how an anonymous Carmelite nun answered these questions almost one hundred years ago:

"A real change in our attitude will only occur when we change the central object of our attention, and when, instead of that object being the self, it comes to be God. When, less and less we find ourselves asking God to work miracles for us, and take instead to asking what we can do for him. When, rather than watching God to see what gift he will produce for us, we begin to wait on God to see what, if anything, we can give to him."

This is how our lives change: by making God the central object of our attention. Not self or success, not pride, greed, lust, envy, gluttony, wrath, or sloth. God.

It makes sense. The more I think about myself, the unhappier I become. The more I make myself available to God, the happier I become. The more I dedicate myself to serving my neighbor, the more my soul is flooded with joy.

What was the central object of your attention when you woke this morning? What will be the central object of your attention when you wake tomorrow? Will your life be changed?

There is a moment during the Mass when the bread and wine are no longer merely bread and wine, but are transformed into the body, blood, soul, and divinity of Jesus Christ. That moment of transformation is unimaginably powerful.

There is a moment in our lives when the central object of our attention is no longer something worldly, when our singular attention shifts, and from that moment on the central object of our attention becomes God. That moment is unimaginably powerful.

I hope and pray with my whole being that this moment is that moment for you.

THE CAUSE OF OUR PAIN

Now you have a decision to make. Will you continue to muddle along in a myriad of worldly desires or will you once and for all set yourself to the definite purpose for which you were created?

The choice is yours.

If you don't choose to wholeheartedly change the central object of your attention, if you choose not to place God at the white-hot center of your heart's desires, you can expect three things will happen.

First, your frustration with life will increase. Without this shift we are discussing, your spiritual progress will be severely limited regardless of what other efforts you make. This is why we often feel like we are spinning our wheels, like we aren't getting anywhere. You could busy yourself twenty-four hours a day with the finest spiritual activities and devotions, but if you don't make God the central object of your attention, you will make very little progress in the spiritual life. And to work so hard and make so little progress will become increasingly frustrating.

Next, you will experience more pain and suffering. This isn't a sadistic wish; it's just an observation of reality. Most of our pain is caused by the gap between what we want and what God wants for us. This pain is the result of the gap between the life we are living and the life we are called to live. When you ignore your conscience in favor of this week's selfish pursuit, you will suffer mental and spiritual anguish. The gap causes pain. You will suffer when the life you are living is out of alignment with what you believe to be good, true, right, and just. When you live a life separated from your values, you suffer. It is impossible for the gap between our will and the will of God to bring about peace, joy, love, and happiness. The gap between the two will always cause pain and suffering.

And finally, you will experience an increasing number of problems.

You'll rush here and there, trying to solve all manner of problems as they arise, but as soon as one appears to be quelled, another will arise. The speed of your life will increase, your frustration at everyone and everything will escalate, and you will gradually lose the ability to enjoy the present moment. You will be too fixated on the next problem that needs solving to enjoy the precious present that God wishes to give you.

All this will be the result of your failure to learn one of the central lessons of life: We are not here to solve the problems; the problems are here to solve us. We all have problems. But the real problem is that we don't understand the role problems are designed to play in our lives. We think we are here to solve the problems. But if you could take inventory of all your problems and solve them overnight, you would awake to new problems in the morning. We are not here to solve the problems; the problems are here to solve us.

This doesn't mean that we sit back and ignore our obligations and let these problems engulf us. It means that we approach problems calmly, we don't rush to solve them, we work to solve them well. This approach to problem solving allows the problems to sharpen our character, to refine our will, to help us to grow in virtue, and to purify us and make us holy.

Let your problems solve you.

THE ONLY TRAGEDY

Your deepest desire—"the desire of your heart" (Psalm 37)—is to become a saint. When I speak to my children about becoming saints, they ask questions that make it clear to me that our times need a different type of saint. But then I am reminded that every age needs a different type of saint. So set aside your resistance and bias based on what you think a saint is and open your heart to new possibilities.

"The only real sadness, the only real failure, the only great tragedy in life, is not to become a saint." These are the words of the French novelist

Léon Bloy.

The nagging feeling we have been discussing seeks to save you from this sadness. That nagging feeling yearns to deliver you from this failure. And that nagging feeling works to help you avert this tragedy.

Your deepest desire is perfectly matched with the purpose of your life.

It makes sense because we have unexplained desires. It explains the dissatisfaction that so often plagues our lives. It is God who gave us those desires, and he yearns to explain our unexplained desires. It is God who created us for more, and he yearns to replace our dissatisfaction with unmitigated fulfillment.

C.S. Lewis observed, "If I find in myself desires which nothing in this world can satisfy, the only logical explanation is that I was made for another world."

Thérèse of Lisieux noted, "God would never inspire me with desires which cannot be realized."

And there is none more famous than Augustine's insight, "You have made us for yourself, O Lord, and our hearts are restless until they rest in you."

It makes sense. The nagging feeling was right all along. You were made for more.

The things of this world are marvelous, and God created them for you to enjoy. But be careful not to love the gift more than the giver of the gift. This is when our priorities begin to get skewed and distorted. This is when the central object of our attention becomes the things of this world.

This world is fabulous, but you weren't made just for this world.

You were made for another world. And if you spend all of your time here on earth living for this world alone, you will never be happy. The only true path to happiness is by following the deepest desire

God has placed in your heart.

Your deepest desire is one that the world won't tell you about because this world cannot fulfill it. If you go into a store to buy new clothes, the salesperson doesn't tell you about an amazing outfit that would be perfect for you and then tell you that he doesn't sell such an outfit. No. The salesperson tries to convince you to buy what he has in the store. And so it is with the world—it is only selling what it has to offer. And as wonderful as those offerings are, they are not enough for you.

When you go to a restaurant, do you read the whole menu? Most people don't. They scan the menu for something familiar. Most of us skip whole sections of the menu. Some people never read the appetizers. Others ignore the list of soups. I became aware recently that I didn't look at the page with salads on it. I just skipped straight over it.

Most people don't even know what's on the menu of life. They choose the first thing that catches their eye and order up a life so much less than the life God dreamed for them. It's time to look at the whole menu.

There is one item on that menu that is worth pursuing more than any other: a life of holiness.

How do you feel about that? Do you feel resistance rising in you? That's okay. Be aware of that resistance but stay with me for just a little longer. The end is worth the wait.

The reason we are resistant to the concept of holiness is twofold: First, we have false conceptions about what it is, and second, we don't believe it is possible. This is the biggest lie in the history of Christianity.

Holiness is the goal of the Christian life. It is the essential purpose of your life. You may have never been told this, but that doesn't make it any less true.

My heart is drawn in this moment to some words I wrote more than twenty-five years ago, in my early twenties, when I was still just beginning this work.

"If you can distract a person from her essential purpose for long enough, she will become miserable. If you can prevent a whole generation from ever discovering their essential purpose, you will create an epidemic of misery and despair."

Isn't this what has happened?

"The greatest tragedy of modern Catholicism is the way we have become so distracted from the goal of the Christian life. My experience has been that the great majority of Catholics do not know the goal of the Christian life. Others have cast the ideal aside, saying it is not conducive to modern living. Tragically, a great many more have never heard it clearly articulated.

"Holiness is the goal of the Christian life.

"Although I am too young to know from firsthand experience, it seems to me that somewhere along the way, a great many educators and priests stopped teaching, preaching, and speaking about this goal. It seems they felt it was an unattainable ideal or simply unrealistic in the changing context of the modern world. They thought it made people feel guilty. They apparently wanted to make it easier for people. So, they threw away or watered down the great goal of the Christian life.

"The result, of course, was exactly the opposite of what they had intended. They didn't make it easier for people; they made it harder for them. Have you ever tried to find your way to a place you have never been before with no directions, no map, and no clear description of the destination?"

It is time to reorient ourselves. We have allowed ourselves to become hypnotized by the complexities of the modern world.

Our faith is simple and beautiful. And it is possible to live it out in new and exciting ways, here and now, in our times. Your personality and circumstances, your needs, talents, and desires, are all gifts to help you live the faith in a deeply personal way.

Holiness is simply the application of the values, principles, and spirit of the Gospel to the circumstances of our everyday lives, one moment at a time. It isn't complicated. It is disarmingly simple.

A new kind of holiness is needed. One that confounds expectations. A new breed of saints. Brave men and women who wholeheartedly embrace the life and teachings of Jesus and live them out creatively.

And here is the good news: Holiness is possible. Anyone who tells you otherwise is confused or a liar, but either way they are absolutely and completely wrong.

Holiness is possible for you. One moment at a time. Set yourself to the task of creating Holy Moments. Don't trouble your heart, mind, and soul with the burden of living a holy life. Each life is a collection of moments. Grasp those moments.

Make God the central object of your attention for one single moment and you will have shifted the momentum of your life. Such is the untapped power that solitary moments hold.

What is a Holy Moment?

A Holy Moment is a single moment in which you open yourself to God. You make yourself available to him. You set aside personal preference and self-interest, and in that one moment, you do what you prayerfully believe God is calling you to do.

Holiness is possible, one moment at a time.

Some moments are holy, some moments are unholy, and you get to decide.

These Holy Moments, these tiny collaborations with God, unleash pure unmitigated joy into our lives. Allow God to flood every corner of your being with that pure unmitigated joy by collaborating with him to create Holy Moments.

Begin today. One of the beautiful things about this idea is that you can implement it immediately. You do not need to study it for years. No special qualifications are necessary. This alone demonstrates the power of the Holy Moments principle.

You are equipped right now to collaborate with God and create Holy Moments. You know everything you need to know right now to begin activating Holy Moments in your life. So, begin today.

And here's the beautiful thing. If you can collaborate with God to create one Holy Moment today, you can create two tomorrow, and four the next day, and eight the day after that. There is no limit to the number of Holy Moments you can participate in.

The want beyond every want is God. We align ourselves with God one moment at a time.

THE UNAVOIDABLE APPOINTMENT

I was just thinking about something I need to do tomorrow. I don't want to do it. Perhaps I will cancel. I have that choice.

There are things in this life that can be avoided and others that are unavoidable. At the top of the list of the unavoidable obligations that we have is an appointment.

That appointment is with death.

Seneca the Younger, the Roman stoic philosopher, wrote a small volume sometime around 49 AD. It was titled *On the Shortness of Life*. He made the case that more than life itself being short, we are wasteful of life.

"People are frugal in guarding their personal property but as soon as it comes to squandering time they are most wasteful of the one thing in which it is right to be stingy.

"It is not that we have a short time to live but that we waste a lot of it. Life is long enough, and a sufficiently generous amount has been given to us for the highest achievements if it were all well invested. But when it is wasted in heedless luxury and spent on no good activity, we are forced at last by death's final constraint to realize that it has

passed away before we knew it was passing. So it is: we are not given a short life, but we make it short, and we are not ill-supplied but wasteful of it ... Life is long if you know how to use it."

Death comes to us all, sooner or later. We don't know when, but we know for certain that it will come. And when it comes it will care nothing for your fame, wealth, education, achievements, possessions, connections, or power.

When death approaches, the person you have become meets the person you could have been. This is a humbling encounter.

Don't wait for death to deliver this encounter. Go out to meet it each day. Spend time each day in the classroom of silence, in communion with God. Meet with the person you are capable of becoming for a few minutes each day in the depths of prayer.

The more time you spend in these meetings the less you will fear death. And these encounters will teach you how to harness your thoughts, words, choices, and actions, to close the gap between who you are today and who you are capable of being.

The deeper you enter into the silence and solitude of these prayerful encounters, the more clearly you will hear the voice of God in your life. He will speak to you through your needs, talents, and desires—and often he will use these ordinary voices to point out the next step in your journey. Resist the temptation to get fixated on what you should do next week or next year. Be content for him to show you your next step.

Just keep taking that next step. One step at a time. Just keep doing the next right thing. This is the way of holiness. This is the path that leads to a deeply fulfilling life. This is the road that will lead you to oneness with God. This union with God is the deepest desire of our hearts—the ultimate want beyond every want.

"Find your delight in the LORD who will give you your heart's desire." (Psalm 37:4)

EPILOGUE:
COME TO THE QUIET

FEAR THE RIGHT THINGS

Our lives are ruled by fear if not by faith.

We fear so many things, but the fears we allow to grip our lives are usually trifles compared to the realities that are worth fearing. At the beginning of this book, I shared with you one of my fears.

I must warn you to begin. I am compelled to tell you something terrifying. We all have fears, but most of us aren't terrified of what should petrify us. Let me tell you what terrifies me. I am petrified of mis-living my life.

You can mis-live your life. Most people never consider it as a possibility, but it's true. We assume that all lives are well-lived. It isn't true. We deceive ourselves.

The disturbing truth is you don't even need to do something significantly egregious. You can do it in the most mundane and ordinary ways. All it takes is the consistent application of mediocrity, laziness, procrastination, self-centeredness, and materialism.

But perhaps the most heartbreaking part of all this is that by mis-living your life you will never get to see or experience the life God envisioned for you. You miss out on the life God wanted to give you. That's heartbreaking.

By listening to the voice of God, we give him the opportunity to steer us toward the life he envisioned for us from the beginning of time.

God gave you needs, talents, and desires to uniquely equip you for the life and mission he created you for. He also speaks to you through prayer and the Sacraments, the Scriptures and the life of the Church, history, prophets, saints and mystics, ordinary people who come into your life, visions and dreams, and the gentle voice within we call conscience.

The mistake we make is listening to all the other voices that shout, whisper, or scream into our lives. Let's take a look at what some of those voices are and how they impact us.

ALL THE OTHER VOICES

There is a story I first heard many years ago that comes to mind this evening as I am finishing this manuscript.

A policeman sees a drunk man searching for something under a street-light and asks what the drunk has lost. The drunk man explains to the policeman that he lost his key.

The policeman, out of compassion, helps the drunk man look for his key. They search feverishly under the streetlight together for the key, but to no avail.

After about fifteen minutes, the policeman asks the drunk if he is sure he dropped the key here by the light post.

"No," the drunk replies, "I think I lost it over there," pointing to a very dark stretch of pavement further down the street.

"Then why are you looking here?" the policeman asks baffled.

"The light is better here," the drunk replies.

The policeman made two mistakes: allowing a drunk to lead the search, and assuming the drunk knew where to search, to begin with.

We all make similar mistakes. We make other mistakes too. Sometimes we go looking for the wrong things, and then it doesn't matter where you look, because even if you find them, they are still the wrong things. But more often than not, we are looking for the right things in the wrong places.

Why are we so enamored with chasing the wrong things? And why do we persistently look for the right things in the wrong places? The answer to these questions is simple and central to our discussion:

We allow ourselves to become confused and distracted by all the other voices in this world. These other voices drown out the quiet voice within us that God uses to direct the daily activity of our lives if we agree to follow his lead.

Ignoring the gentle voice within—the voice of conscience—is the origins of all my regrets. Setting God's voice aside and listening to all the other voices has always been a recipe for disaster, and yet, we continue to choose that path on a daily basis.

Noise is the spiritual violence of our age. The world just keeps getting louder.

Every day we are bombarded with the voices of these supposed "experts" and "influencers" with competing ideas, opinions, and agendas. They assault every aspect of our lives and seek to influence every decision. They talk to us about our personal finances, career choices, relationships, education decisions, how to raise children, what to eat, where to shop, what to buy, what music to listen to and books to read, which political ideas should be front and center on our minds, which candidates are worthy of our votes, and all the reasons religion is bad and faith is a relic of the past. These interactions tend to leave us angry, confused, anxious, afraid, and overwhelmed—and yet we keep coming back for more each day.

These are conversations we should be having with God and people who are striving to "live justly, love tenderly, and walk humbly with God." (Micah 6:8)

Come to think of it, isn't that a good litmus test for the people we should listen to? Who would you watch on television if you only tuned in to people who are striving to "live justly, love tenderly, and walk humbly with God"? Which podcasts would you listen to? Which books would you read? And what movies and television shows would you watch?

These are unsettling questions because they reveal how much airtime we give to unfaithful ideas and voices in our lives.

And then there are the big five. The big five refers to the five people in your life with whom you spend the most time. It has been observed that people emulate the five people they spend the most time with—for better or for worse.

There are plenty of successful businesspeople whose five closest friends are also successful businesspeople. And plenty of physically fit people whose five closest friends are health fanatics. And it's amazing how many of the saints had friends who are also canonized saints.

How would you describe your five closest friends? What are their values and priorities? Do they align with how you feel called to live your life? Do they help you become a-better-version-of-yourself? Or do they fill your life with gossip and toxic ideas that lead you away from God?

These five people have very influential voices in your life whether you are aware of it or not.

The world is full of voices and the great majority should be ignored. The easiest way to mis-live your life is to limit the amount of time you spend listening to the voice of God and maximize the time you spend listening to all these other voices.

If we listen to the advice of fools, we will become fools ourselves. If we pour toxic content into our hearts and minds, our hearts and minds will become toxic.

To live a rich and fulfilling mission-driven life you need wise counsel, and there is none wiser than the counsel of God.

COME TO THE QUIET

"We will make the whole universe a noise in the end."

These are the words C. S. Lewis prophetically placed in the mouth of the devil almost one hundred years ago. His famous collection of letters between the senior devil, Screwtape, and his apprentice, Wormwood, were both humorous and insightful.

The thirty-one letters were later published in a book titled *The Screwtape Letters*. In the letters, Screwtape is advising Wormwood about the procedure for winning a soul away from God for the devil. At one point, Wormwood is trying to think up all kinds of creative and exotic ways to tempt the man who has been assigned to him, and Screwtape rebukes him, explaining that their methods have long been established. One such method, he explains, is simply to create so much noise that men and women can no longer hear the voice of God in their lives.

Can you hear the voice of God in your life?

Written one hundred years ago, before the invention of most of the contraptions that assault our lives with constant noise today, C. S. Lewis presented a prophetic vision of the diabolical role noise plays in our lives.

This idea of creating so much noise that people can no longer hear the voice of God in their lives is so simple and so diabolical and it is exactly what has happened.

It is for this reason that I close these pages with an invitation.

Come to the quiet.

It is the panacea of our times.

Silence is a healing balm for the modern soul. I cannot recommend it to you enough. Come to the quiet. Rest in God's eternal silence and allow him to soothe your soul. Allow him to calm your mind and still your soul.

Never underestimate the power of silence. Simply by increasing the amount of time you spend in silence you give God the opportunity to radically alter the direction of your life.

You need stillness, silence, and solitude. You desire stillness, silence, and solitude.

Come to the quiet. Set a specific time each day and allot a specific amount of time to remain with God in the silence.

Come to the quiet. This is the simplest and most natural way to establish God as the central object of your attention.

Come to the quiet. God speaks in the silence. If you yearn to hear his voice, increase the amount of time you spend in silence each day, and wait patiently for him to speak to you.

Come to the quiet.

Allow God to speak to you through your needs, talents, and desires.

Come to the quiet.

This is a beautiful countercultural act.

Come to the quiet.

This is an otherworldly activity.

Come to the quiet.

Just because you are lost doesn't mean your compass is broken.

Come to the quiet.